Mustang Aces of the 357th Fighter Group

SERIES EDITOR: TONY HOLMES

OSPREY AIRCRAFT OF THE ACES • 96

Mustang Aces of the 357th Fighter Group

Chris Bucholtz

OSPREY
PUBLISHING

Front Cover
On 18 September 1944 the 357th Fighter Group (FG) was aloft as part of the fighter cover for the supply drops of Operation *Market Garden* (the airborne assault on the Netherlands) when it ran headlong into a large number of German fighters. Lt Gerald Tyler, a native of Sarasota, Florida, was leading a flight of Mustangs from the 364th Fighter Squadron (FS) in his P-51D-10 44-14660 *LITTLE DUCKFOOT* when he spotted the enemy aircraft, and as he turned to attack them he 'saw the sun glistening off other bandits above them'. Climbing to attack the top cover, he was bounced by eight Fw 190s but quickly turned the tables on them. Meeting the formation leader and head-on, Tyler fired a long burst and 'saw strikes all over the fuselage and centre section. He began burning and went straight down past me into the ground'.

After covering another Mustang as it downed a Luftwaffe fighter, he caught a Bf 109 in a turning fight, and following several tight turns, drew deflection and opened fire, sending the Messerschmitt into a spin wreathed in flames. A third German fighter dove at his flight but Tyler had soon got in behind this aircraft too, chasing it down to the deck and firing 'until the smoke was so thick that I could no longer see him'. The Bf 109 crashed into a stand of trees north of the Dutch city of Maastricht for Tyler's seventh, and final, kill. In all, the 357th scored 26 victories on the first day of *Market Garden*, and added 24 more on 19 September during sweeps over Holland (*Cover artwork by Mark Postlethwaite*)

Dedication
This book is dedicated to the memory of Merle Olmstead, the true keeper of the tale of the 357th FG.

First published in Great Britain in 2010 by Osprey Publishing
Midland House, West Way, Botley, Oxford, OX2 0PH, UK
44-02 23rd St, Suite 219, Long Island City, NY 11101, USA

E-mail: info@ospreypublishing.com

ISBN 13: 978 1 84603 985 0
E-book ISBN: 978 1 84603 986 7

Edited by Tony Holmes and Bruce Hales-Dutton
Page design by Tony Truscott
Cover Artwork by Mark Postlethwaite
Aircraft Profiles by Chris Davey
Index by Alan Thatcher
Originated by PDQ Digital Media Solutions
Printed and bound in China through Bookbuilders

10 11 12 13 14 15   10 9 8 7 6 5 4 3 2 1

Osprey Publishing is supporting the Woodland Trust, the UK's leading woodland conservation charity by funding the dedication of trees.

www.ospreypublishing.com

ACKNOWLEDGEMENTS
This book owes much to Jim Roeder whose generosity accounts for many of the photographs. Also, thanks to Jeff Bomstead of the Northwestern Friends of the Aces and to Peter Randall, whose Littlefriends.co.uk website collects a priceless wealth of information in one place. Special thanks go to my loving wife who coped with my fevered editing with bemused toleration.

CONTENTS

FROM CALIFORNIA TO 'BIG WEEK'

On 1 December 1942, nearly a year after the United States entered World War 2, the US Army Air Forces (USAAF) ordered the 357th Fighter Group (FG) into existence at Hamilton Field, California. No one could know at the time that this order had created the Eighth Air Force's greatest ace-making unit. In just over a year of combat 42 pilots would achieve 'acedom' flying with the 357th FG – more than any other unit in Europe.

Three squadrons – the 362nd, 363rd and 364th FSs – were established under the command of Col Loring Stetson, and during the first two months of the group's existence it was outfitted with everything it would need for operations except for one crucial item – aircraft. In February 1943 the group travelled to Tonopah, Nevada, which was home to a three-million acre bombing and gunnery range. Training began immediately with Bell P-39D/Q Airacobras that had been left behind by the 354th FG. Flight leaders in each squadron did much of the training, and among their number were a handful of future aces including the 362nd's Joseph Broadhead, the 363rd's Clarence 'Bud' Anderson, Edwin Hiro and William O'Brien and the 364th's John Storch, Jack Warren and Glendon Davis.

The P-39 proved to be a challenge to fly at altitude, and Tonopah, situated some 6000 ft above sea level, placed the fighter at a disadvantage from the start. The aircraft had a reputation for tumbling around its centre of gravity, and the fighter also tended to stall suddenly – a dangerous attribute for neophyte fighter pilots. Two pilots were killed at Tonopah in P-39s, but most painful was the loss of Capt Varian White, commander of the 364th and a veteran of combat in the Pacific. White flew from Tonopah to Burbank to visit his fiancé's parents, but on his return trip on 18 May his Airacobra suffered an engine failure shortly

One of the 357th FG's training bases was Oroville, in California, where this 363rd FS P-39D was photographed. The squadron's original, and unofficial, logo is featured prominently on the fighter's cockpit door (*USAF*)

after take-off and crashed into a house in Studio City.

In June the group returned to California. Accidents increased as the pilots gained confidence, with nine more being killed during June and July. The latter month also saw the departure of Lt Col Stetson, who was sent to North Africa to command the P-40-equipped 33rd FG. He was replaced by Lt Col Edwin Chickering. The group lost two more pilots in August and September.

Another accident, this time on the ground, jeopardised the career of a future ace when Lt Alfred Boyle accidentally fired his 0.45-cal pistol and put a bullet through the upper right arm of 363rd FS pilot Lt William O'Brien. The bullet missed the bone but caused nerve damage, and a month later O'Brien's hand was still not working properly. Nevertheless, he travelled with the group to England, where he was evaluated again. It was recommended that he should be transferred back to the US and discharged, but the doctor's recommendation was not heeded and O'Brien was allowed to fly, although during the first few months of combat he had to use his left hand to fire his guns.

In the first week of October 1943 the three squadrons moved east – the 362nd to Idaho, the 363rd to Wyoming and the 364th to Nebraska – for a month of familiarisation flying with bombers, and for more combat training. Late in the month, the group was ordered to head to Camp Shanks, New York, and on the 23rd its personnel embarked on board RMS *Queen Elizabeth* for the ship's next trip from New York to Britain. Left behind were the group's P-39s, but waiting for them in England were the aircraft with which they would make history – North American P-51 Mustangs.

After just six days at sea, the *Queen Elizabeth* arrived in the Firth of Clyde, and a short while later the men of the 357th headed for Raydon Wood airfield, in Suffolk. The group's first aircraft arrived in the second week of December in the shape of an L-4 Cub, but the real excitement came on the 19th of the month when a well-worn ex-RAF Mustang III flew in. By the end December, 14 more Merlin-powered P-51Bs had been delivered, and just prior to the group flying its first mission – on 14 January 1944 – a fresh batch of fighters brought it up to strength.

On that date Col Chickering, accompanied by Majs Don Graham and Hubert Egenes, flew with the P-51B-equipped 354th FG on a mission over Germany. Another mission with the latter unit, on 24 January, saw Capts Joseph Giltner, Joseph Broadhead, Ed Hiro and John Storch accompanying the 'Pioneer Mustang Group' into action, but Giltner's flight was bounced by Fw 190s near Antwerp and he was shot down to become a prisoner of war (PoW). Giltner, flying a 354th FG P-51B, had claimed a Focke-Wulf fighter destroyed minutes prior to his demise, however.

An administrative change on 1 February transferred the 357th

The 362nd FS counted these P-39Ls among its training aircraft during the unit's time at Hayward, in California. The squadron's machines each bore names in small letters chalked just below the numbers on the nose (*Olmsted via Roeder*)

Future ace Lt William O'Brien thought the flight characteristics of the Airacobra were 'truly the definition of a bitch', hence the name he gave his P-39Q. His next two mounts, also named *BILLY'S BITCH*, were a P-51B and a P-51D, which were presumably better behaved (*Olmsted via Roeder*)

Tape was used to seal the seams during the Mustangs' transatlantic shipment, thus protecting them from salt water corrosion. Pictured here closest to the camera, Maj Don Graham's P-51B-5 shows how removal of the tape lifted the paint on the early aircraft. The ace Lt Joe Pierce was at the fighter's controls when 43-6712 was wrecked in a taxiing accident at Leiston on 25 April 1944. Pierce's assigned aircraft was 43-6644, which is the machine immediately behind Maj Graham's fighter. The ace claimed at least one kill with this P-51B, on 12 May. The third aircraft in the line is Lt Richard Peterson's P-51B-5 43-6935 *Hurry Home Honey*. Each of the aircraft is carrying a pair of early style 75-gallon drop tanks (*Olmsted via Roeder*)

from Ninth Air Force control to the Eighth Air Force, as the latter needed long-range fighters to escort its B-17s and B-24s. In exchange, the Ninth received the P-47-equipped 358th FG. The swap also included bases, with the 358th moving to Raydon Wood and the 357th going to Station F-373, which was located between the Suffolk towns of Leiston, Saxmundham and Theberton. The presence of a new American Mustang group in the Eighth Air Force did not escape the attentions of the Nazi propaganda machine. Indeed, during one of his broadcasts 'Lord Haw-Haw' began referring to the group as the 'Yoxford Boys' in a reference to a small town which was actually further away from the base than the other trio of towns mentioned above. Yet the nickname had a ring to it and the group adopted it as its own.

INTO ACTION

On 11 February the 357th FG flew its first official mission in the form of a sweep to the Rouen area, led by ace and recent Medal of Honor recipient Maj James Howard of the 354th FG. The next day another veteran fighter leader, and ace, Lt Col Don Blakeslee of the 4th FG led a bomber escort for Eighth Air Force 'heavies' sent to attack *No Ball* (V1) sites in France. Blakeslee also headed up a second sweep over the Dieppe area on 13 February. Eighth Air Force activity was curtailed by bad weather for the following six days, allowing preparations to be made for Operation *Argument* – a six-day attack on the German aircraft industry that also offered an opportunity to destroy the Luftwaffe in the air. On 17 February Col Chickering was moved to the Eighth Air Force staff and Col Henry Spicer was given command of the 357th.

The hard-charging Spicer flew as Blakeslee's wingman on 20 February during an escort mission to Leipzig. The group scored its first victories when, north of the target, several Messerschmitt fighters went after Lt Calvert Williams' 362nd FS flight. One of the Bf 109s overshot and Williams promptly sent it down in a cloud of black smoke. Williams also saw Lt Donald Ross of the 363rd FS shoot down a second Bf 109, but Ross' P-51B in turn flew through some of the debris and he was forced to bail out to become a PoW.

The next day, Spicer led an escort mission to Braunschweig, and the group scored another victory that also cost it a pilot. Lt Alfred Boyle latched on to a Bf 109 in a dive,

Future 363rd FS aces Capt 'Bud' Anderson and Lt Jim Browning pose beside Anderson's first *OLD CROW*, P-51B-5 43-6723. This aircraft was being flown by Lt Al Boyle on 21 February 1944 when he shot down a Bf 109, but the American fighter was in turn hit by debris from the disintegrating Messerschmitt and *OLD CROW* crashed near Meppel. Boyle spent the rest of the war as a PoW (*Olmsted via Roeder*)

closing in to 50 yards. With the two fighters travelling at an estimated 600 mph, the Bf 109 disintegrated and bits of it severely damaged Boyle's Mustang. He also bailed out into captivity.

On 22 February, during an escort mission to Bernberg, the group made a late rendezvous with the bombers, catching them only after they had reached their initial point. Spicer took his 11 aircraft to the front of the formation, intercepting six Bf 109s preparing to attack the bombers head-on. The group CO later recalled;

'This attack was broken up, one of the '109s breaking over me. I hauled my Mustang around in a tight turn and gave chase. I closed from dead astern and below, waited until he filled the sight, and gave him the "Gen Kepner one-two". He immediately blew up and became obscured in a brownish-orange cloud of smoke. I pulled up and passed over him with little more than ten feet between us, and I distinctly recall seeing the black crosses on the wings. I then rolled over to watch him go down. The ship completed a 180-degree diving turn, levelled off and, as it didn't seem to be on fire, I took off after him again. But before I could close the second time he began flopping, turned over and dove straight down. I could see his shadow rapidly coming in from the south, and as the two merged, a beautiful explosion took place, sullying the otherwise tranquil and pastoral snowscape with vivid red flame and billowing black smoke.'

Despite the 357th FG's timely intervention, the enemy fighters nevertheless made a pass at the bombers. 364th FS pilot, and future five-kill ace, Capt Jack Warren of San Jacinto, California, closed on one of the Messerschmitts and fired a short burst, 'which seemed to hit the cockpit and the aeroplane started a steeper dive to the left. I fired several bursts at about 300 to 400 yards and observed smoke trailing. I pulled out at about 5000 ft and circled. I saw the Me 109 go into the ground and explode.'

Squadronmate, and future seven-kill ace, Lt John Carder identified a diving Bf 109G, dived after it and fired at 600 yards. He reported;

'I believe I got a few strikes, causing the left landing gear to partially extend. I lost sight of him, and found him again going through some clouds in a long straight dive. I split-ess'ed onto his tail and fired three bursts from 400 yards down to 100 yards or less. The first two bursts

Capt 'Walrus Jack' Warren of the 364th FS was the second pilot in the 357th FG to 'make ace' on 16 March 1944 when he claimed three kills in a single mission. Just 48 hours later he was lost in bad weather near Ostend (*Olmsted via Roeder*)

Col Henry Spicer and his crew pose with P-51B-5 43-6880 *TONY BOY*, in which the group CO scored three kills (one on 22 February 1944 and two more 48 hours later). Spicer was well on his way to becoming an ace when, while flying this machine on 5 March 1944, his cooling system was damaged by flak and he had to bail out over the Channel southwest of Le Havre. Spicer became a PoW, and a constant thorn in the side of his captors (*Olmsted via Roeder*)

had no effect. The third got him and he blew up as I passed over him. Debris damaged my spinner and the blast blistered paint and burnt the fabric on my elevator.'

In all, the group scored seven victories, but lost two fighters and pilots. Warren and Carder did not know it at the time but they were the group's first aces to draw blood.

The 357th FG was over Germany again on 24 February, escorting bombers to Gotha. Near Koblenz, the 364th FS spotted enemy aircraft below them, and Capt John Medieros and wingman, and future 15.5-kill ace, Lt Richard 'Pete' Peterson split-ess'ed to get onto their tails. According to Medieros, 'the enemy aircraft tried skidding and small turns to evade us, but to no avail. When he quit skidding I gave him a burst and observed strikes on the left wing root. The next burst was short and the third short burst hit him square on the tail. I had to pull up to avoid running into the debris'. As Medieros pulled away, Peterson noted that 'the aeroplane blew up in to a ball of red fire and smoke'.

Spicer and his wingman then spotted two Bf 109s, although the German fighters escaped. Moments later the two Americans pilots saw a Ju 88 below them. Spicer gave chase, and later reported;

'He went down fast, losing altitude in a steep spiral. At about 3000 ft I turned tight inside of him and he obligingly straightened out, allowing me to do the same, so I closed and opened fire at about 600 yards in an attempt to discourage the rear gunner. Steady fire was held until he burst into flames. I overran him rapidly so I yanked it out to the side to watch the fun. The whole aeroplane was coming unbuttoned. My wingman, Henry Beal, saw two men jump and their 'chutes open (poor shooting on my part). The ship continued straight ahead, diving at an angle of about 40 degrees until contact with Mother Earth was made, which caused the usual splendid spectacle of smoke and flame.

'Looking up suddenly, lo and behold if there wasn't an Me 110 dashing across the horizon. He showed a little sense and tried not to turn, so I was forced to resort to deflection shooting, opening up and spraying him up and down, round and across. Fortunately, the left engine blew up and burst into flames. As I overran him, still indicating 500 mph, the pilot dumped the canopy and started to get out. He was dressed in brown and had streaming yellow hair, the handsome devil. No 'chute was seen, but the aircraft descended impolitely into the centre of the town of Erfurt, causing rather understandable confusion as it blew up and burned merrily.'

On 25 February the group was part of an escort to Regensburg. Future eight-kill ace Capt Joseph Broadhead and his wingman Lt Thomas Beemer spotted a solitary Bf 109 2000 ft above the B-17s. Lt Gilbert O'Brien had a ringside seat;

'Just about the time Capt Broadhead fired a burst, the Me 109 peeled off into the bombers. Capt

Broadhead and Lt Beemer followed him into the formation. Then I saw Lt Beemer's ship start smoking. I saw him make three 360-degree gliding turns down to 15,000 ft. I followed the two P-51s through the bombers and saw every turret on the B-17s smoking and winking at me.'

Beemer had been hit by the bombers' fire and soon had to bail out of his fighter, but his parachute failed to open properly and he plummeted to earth. His fall was broken by a clump of trees, however, and the badly injured Beemer was duly repatriated by the Germans several months later.

Meanwhile, Broadhead finally overhauled the enemy fighter, but the Bf 109 pilot 'saw me and made a quick bank to the left. I closed fast to within 50 yards and observed strikes on his engine and right wing. He reversed direction and split-ess'ed to the right. He then pulled out at 15,000 ft, rolled twice to the left and began a shallow dive. I fired continually, hitting him throughout the manoeuvre. As soon as he began his dive the aircraft started disintegrating. Cowling, canopy and various parts flew off.'

Future 362nd FS ace Lt Bob Becker also enjoyed success on this mission, with 1.5 Bf 110s destroyed.

It was not until 2 March that the group saw action again, with 364th FS CO and future 8.5-kill ace Maj Thomas Hayes leading it north of Frankfurt. Hayes had flown P-40s with the 17th Pursuit Squadron (Provisional) against the Japanese in Java and had been shot down on 20 February 1942 over Bali. Now he was anxious for revenge on the Axis. Hayes spotted two Bf 109s that 'must have attacked the rear of the box'. He later recalled;

'We dropped our auxiliary tanks and started down, having several thousand feet on them. Still not in range, they split at about 9000 ft, with me and my wingman taking the leader, who kept a straight course in a gradual dive. I started to fire at about 350 yards. Very few strikes were observed. At 1000 ft I was firing dead astern and had his engine smoking. Suddenly, he dumped almost straight down and crashed in a wooded area. The pilot crashed with the aeroplane, and I believe he was hit from the astern attack through his armour plate.'

Lt John Carder and wingman (future 5.5-kill ace) Lt LeRoy Ruder stalked the second fighter, which, the former reported, 'went into a valley with a steep tree-lined hill on the far side. At the bottom of the hill I fired a burst and saw strikes on the right wing. The Me 109 pulled up sharply above the horizon and I saw his wingtip was crumpled. I believe he hit a tree, unless I had damaged his wing spar. He did a slow climbing half roll and went down, again inverted, and crashed on top of the hill. I could see part of the wing and a wheel that slid into the main street of the town. I did a roll, and believe civilian morale is lower now.'

Lt Robert Becker's first mount was P-51B-5 43-6783, which initially displayed just the tiger's head logo but later bore the name *Sebastian*. Becker scored his first victories in this aircraft on 25 February 1944, when he downed a Bf 110 and shared in the destruction of a second *Zerstörer*. Both aircraft were attacked over Regensburg (*Olmsted via Roeder*)

BERLIN BOUND

On 3 March the 357th FG was assigned the target everyone had been waiting for – Berlin. After pilots had rendezvoused with the bombers, however, the mission was aborted because of bad weather. The group still managed to lose a Mustang nevertheless when the engine of future ace Lt Robert Foy's P-51B failed on the way home and he bailed out over the Channel. Fellow future ace Lt Howard Hively of the 4th FG, who was himself a survivor of a Channel bail-out, heard the distress calls and made a low-level search. He located Foy in his dinghy and circled over him until an RAF Air-Sea Rescue Walrus arrived. The latter directed a high-speed launch to the scene and Foy was rescued, unharmed except for a mild case of shock.

The following day's target was also Berlin. Again the weather was bad, but the 500 B-17s carried on. While racing to rendezvous with the bombers, the 357th saw other Mustangs returning to England. Much of the force – bombers as well as fighters – had heard a recall signal, the authenticity of which historians still debate. Just 29 B-17s pressed on for Berlin and, shielded by cloud, they hit the target without seeing German fighters. After bombing, however, the Luftwaffe appeared and, out of the clouds, so did the Mustangs.

Southeast of Kassel, the 363rd FS's White Flight spotted a Bf 109 to the right and behind them. Flying as a member of the flight was future 11.5-victory ace Flt Off Charles 'Chuck' Yeager. A West Virginian of humble origin, Yeager had joined the US Army in 1941 and served as an aircraft mechanic before the USAAF began admitting flight trainees without a college degree. When the opportunity presented itself, Yeager applied for flight training and, with his extraordinary eyesight, proved to be a natural for fighters.

Ever the opportunist, Yeager broke into the Bf 109. The enemy fighter, displaying a large red and black devil's head logo on its side, turned right and went into a 50-degree dive. Yeager takes up the story;

'I closed up fast and opened fire at 200 yards. I observed strikes on the fuselage and wing roots, with pieces flying off. I was over-running so I pulled up and did an aileron roll and fell in behind again and started shooting at 150 yards. The enemy aircraft's engine was smoking and windmilling. I overran again, observing strikes on the fuselage and canopy. I pulled up again and did a wingover on his tail. His canopy flew off and the pilot bailed out.'

More than 200 B-24s bombed airfields near Bordeaux on 5 March. East of the target the 363rd FS's Green Flight sighted three Bf 109s moving in behind the bombers. Lt Ellis Rogers, the flight leader, put his Mustangs behind this trio. He subsequently reported;

'We closed to approximately 250 yards, where we were apparently seen, for they added throttle and broke before we could fire. Two went up to the right and the third went down to the left, and we followed him. I closed to approximately 150 yards and fired several bursts, correcting my aim as I saw numerous strikes on the left wing, tail and fuselage. The pilot bailed out at approximately 5000 ft.'

Rogers also shared a second kill with Lts Charles Peters and Don Bochkay, but he was subsequently killed on 8 May when his Mustang shed a wing. The pilots with whom he shared his victory would both go on to achieve ace status, however.

After the bomb run Spicer despatched one flight of the 363rd FS to escort straggling B-24s. It consisted of Lts William O'Brien, Bob Moore, William McGinley and Flt Off Yeager, who took up station on the bombers' right side. Almost immediately, a Bf 109 tried to attack from behind. 'Yeager's call saved us all', stated O'Brien after the mission. Following the break more fighters were spotted, and O'Brien tagged onto an Fw 190 in a diving turn. He opened fire at close range, knocking pieces off the fighter. 'Both of us were diving nearly vertical when something large went flying past my cockpit'. It was the German pilot, Imfred Klotz, whose parachute failed to open.

Then a call came over the radio. 'Hi fellas. I just got hit and have to bail out!' It was Yeager, who had been shot up moments earlier by the Focke-Wulf that O'Brien had just clobbered. Later, Yeager linked up with the French Resistance and would eventually make it back to England via Spain. Despite regulations requiring pilots who had been in contact with the Resistance to be transferred out of theatre in case they were captured again and revealed information to the Germans, Yeager took his case to the Supreme Allied Commander. Gen Dwight Eisenhower passed the request to Washington, D.C., but while the bureaucratic machinery was turning Yeager remained in a state of limbo.

The 364th FS's Lt Richard Peterson downed an Fw 190 near the target to achieve his first victory, and on the way home his unit found even more unusual game. 'Through a hole in the clouds, Capt Glendon Davis spotted three large aircraft taking off from a field near Parthenay', reported future five-kill ace Lt Morris Stanley. As they approached they identified the aircraft as Fw 200 Condors. At just 200 ft off the deck, Davis reached firing range and peppered the first Fw 200. 'As he pulled up to avoid a collision, I noticed the left landing gear of the enemy aircraft fall down', Stanley said. The Fw 200 soon crashed, 'first ground looping, then cartwheeling until it was wrecked'. The P-51 pilots closed in on two more Fw 200s, Stanley describing what happened next;

'Capt Davis fired a long burst. I observed strikes on the wings and engine nacelles followed by flame and smoke from the No 3 engine. As Davis pulled up, I closed to 250 yards behind the remaining ship and started firing from dead astern, and I continued to fire to approximately 25 yards, observing strikes on the wings and fuselage.'

Stanley saw Davis' second Focke-Wulf crash and burn, 'and a few seconds later I noticed the Fw 200 that I had shot at start a slow turn to the left and hit the ground and explode'.

As the group was heading for home, flak damaged Col Spicer's fighter. 'The colonel told me he was going to bail out after riding it as far as he could over the water', said his wingman, future six-kill ace Lt John Pugh. Spicer's aircraft caught fire and he bailed out. Rescue efforts failed and he drifted in his dinghy for two days before being washed ashore, suffering from frostbite and exposure. Enemy soldiers

Lt Charles Peters of the 353rd FS was credited with 3.33 victories. He shared in Don Bochkay's first kill on 5 March 1944, then achieved his first solo victory on 11 April, with a second on 19 May over Berlin. He was sitting in another pilot's aircraft when this photograph was taken, hence the scoreboard (*Cook via Randall*)

found him, and he was taken to Oberursel, in Germany, for recuperation and questioning, including several sessions with expert Luftwaffe interrogator Hans Scharff. The latter reported that Spicer was adept at not revealing information.

The colonel was soon sent to *Stalag Luft* I in Barth, where he became senior officer of North Compound No 2 and a constant thorn in the side of the German guards. One cold morning in October the guards could not get the prisoner roll call correct, and after two hours of failed tallies Spicer ordered the PoWs to ignore the guards and return to their barracks. Later, the colonel gathered the men in the compound and addressed them in a loud voice, intending his words reach German ears as well as those of his own men. 'Remember', he said, 'we are still at war with the Germans. They are dirty lying sneaks and can't be trusted'. Spicer continued with tales of Germans machine gunning wounded soldiers and murdering civilians, before concluding, 'They're a bunch of murderous, no-good liars and if we have to stay here for 15 years to see all the Germans killed then it'll be worth it'. The PoWs erupted in cheers.

The gurads' reaction was less enthusiastic. Spicer was confined to a small cell awaiting a court martial for 'defaming German character' and 'inciting prisoners to riot'. The court sentenced him to six months in solitary confinement followed by execution by firing squad. In April 1945, with the Russians driving deeper into Germany, the guards abandoned the camp, but when Spicer was told he was free he refused to leave his cell. 'I have one more night to make it an even six months', he said. After emerging the next morning he was enthusiastically cheered by his fellow PoWs. Spicer remained in the air force for another 19 years and retired as a major general.

The group again visited Berlin on 6 March. Among the 15 pilots to abort was the new group commander, Lt Col Don Graham, who placed 364th CO Maj Tommy Hayes in charge. The continent was completely blanketed by cloud, hampering navigation. At the designated time for

The 357th FG's paint schemes were idiosyncratic in the main, but Lt John Pugh's P-51B-10 42-106473 *Geronimo* featured the most outlandish. In late March 1944 it was adorned with a yellow nose and red diamonds, which may have been due to a misreading of the directive for red and yellow checkerboards to be applied to the nose as a group marking. In any event, this scheme was probably not displayed on aircraft used in combat over Europe (*Olmsted via Roeder*)

Capt William 'Obee' O'Brien 'made ace' by downing two Bf 109s east of Schonesbeck on 30 May 1944, despite nerve damage from a pre-deployment gunshot wound that forced him to fire his guns using his left hand (*Olmsted via Roeder*)

rendezvous with the bombers Hayes broke radio silence, asking Capt William O'Brien 'Where's Berlin, "Obee"?' O'Brien radioed back, 'I think Berlin's behind us'. The group made a 180-degree turn without seeing a break in the clouds. However, as the fighters' completed their turn the bombers broke out of the clouds seven miles away and just to the left. Before anyone could exult in the near-perfect rendezvous, another voice broke in. '"Bogies", "two" and "three o'clock level"!' More than 100 German aircraft were heading for the bombers, led by seven Bf 110s of III./NJG 5 commanded by Major Hans Kogler. And behind Kogler's nightfighters were 41 Me 410s and 72 Bf 109s.

'The Me 110 that I latched onto was easy pickings, which was okay with me', O'Brien noted later. 'I got him burning in his left engine area and we were in a very steep diving right turn when my machine guns started jamming'. As he tried to clear his weapons the Bf 110 dived vertically, smashing into what O'Brien described as a building resembling a factory. 'You never saw such a fine explosion'. Hayes, meanwhile, went for the top cover flight of four Bf 109s, separating one from the rest and turning with him until the pilot decided to dive away. Hayes went after him, but lost his quarry in the smoke of battle and levelled off. As he looked around he saw B-17s massed above him with their bomb-bay doors open. Rather than be pelted with 500 'pounders', Hayes peeled off and wound up at 500 ft on a parallel course, seeing the bombs exploding in his rear-view mirror. He climbed out and rejoined his flight.

Capt LeRoy Ruder was flying as Lt John Carder's wingman and he also attacked a Bf 110. 'Carder overshot and I fired a burst from close range that blew the canopy to pieces and must have killed the pilot', Ruder noted in his diary. 'The aeroplane went into a steep dive from 20,000 ft and we followed it down to 5000 ft, where Capt William O'Brien fired at it until it burst into flames'. Carder and Ruder soon saw a Bf 109 attacking a B-17 whose crew was bailing out. Even though only one gun on O'Brien's P-51 was working by then, he still went after the Bf 109, chasing it to the deck. 'I didn't observe strikes on this aircraft and make no claim', O'Brien wrote. 'I did scare the hell out of it though'.

His Mustang's guns jammed, O'Brien formed up with Ruder for the flight home. A few minutes later, Ruder called a 'bogie' at 'two o'clock' – another Bf 110 armed with rockets that was still trying to get a shot at the bombers. O'Brien told Ruder to take it. 'I attacked from dead astern at about 200 to 150 yards and hit the left engine', said Ruder. 'I next fired at the fuselage and right engine, striking both of them. I had only one gun firing at the time, but it did the job. Oil from the enemy aircraft covered my canopy and he fell away in a spin, with both engines smoking badly'. The Bf 110 managed to crash-land, however, and its pilot, Leutnant G Wolf, survived the encounter.

As Hayes' flight headed for home he spotted a single Bf 109 flying in the opposite direction a few miles to his right. Hayes reversed his course and held his fire until he had closed to 200 yards. Strikes sparkled around the cockpit area and the Bf 109 lurched into a dive, exploding when it hit the ground and killing Unteroffizier K Pelz of JG 302. Shortly afterwards, another member of Hayes' flight, Lt John Howell, spotted a Bf 109 flown by Oberleutnant Gerhard Loos, a 92-kill ace and *staffelkapitän* of 8./JG 54. Howell opened fire and overshot Loos, but Carder closed in to finish off the German ace. The latter may have bailed out before this attack, but in attempting to avoid power lines he fell out of his parachute and plummeted 70 ft to his death.

After each of them had downed a Bf 110, Capt Davis and his wingman, future five-kill ace Lt Tom Harris, were heading home when they spotted a B-17 straggler with an Fw 190 on its tail. Davis reported;

'We dove down on the enemy aircraft but couldn't close on him as the tail gunner of the bomber was firing at him. We broke to the side of the enemy aircraft, and at that time he saw us and broke into us. We turned into him and he dived for the deck in a tight spiral. We followed him down, indicating from 450 mph to 500 mph. At 10,000 ft he dropped his belly tank. At 5000 ft his aeroplane appeared to be stalling as he tried to pull out. His canopy flew off but the aeroplane went right into the ground without the pilot getting out.'

In all, the group had scored 20 kills – including victories for future aces Don Bochkay, Joe Broadhead and Morris Stanley, as well as a half kill for Arval Roberson – without a single loss. It had been the first of what would be many big days for the 357th FG.

On 8 March the group again set off for Berlin as escorts for B-24s sent to attack the VKF ball bearings plant. As they neared the target, Lt Col Graham's lead flight saw German fighters shoot down a Liberator. Diving after the enemy aircraft, Carder reported;

'The colonel and his wingman, Lt Peterson, took after two of them while my wingman, Lt Hollis Nowlin, and I went after the third. I fired a burst from 300 yards at 40 degrees deflection and got strikes on the engine and canopy, killing the pilot I believe. The Fw 190 then rolled onto its back in a steep climb, with the engine emitting black puffs of smoke. I continued firing from an inverted position from 100 yards astern, observing strikes. I pulled back to 5000 ft as the enemy aircraft crashed below me.'

Meanwhile, Blue Flight of the 364th was orbiting Dummer Lake waiting for Hayes to rejoin when an Fw 190 flew past the Mustangs. Capt 'Glen' Davis recalled;

'I called to Maj Hayes that I was attacking him and caught him on the deck after about three minutes. He saw me coming, and when I was 500 yards away he pulled up and turned into me. I turned into him and he swung around, almost getting on the tail of Lt Irving Smith, who was following me. I called to him to put down flaps and turn with him, as I had 20-degree of flap myself.

'We went around five or six times, with the issue very much in doubt. I couldn't get quite enough deflection to nail him, though I was firing short bursts trying to get him to roll out, which he was too smart to do. I also observed Lt Harris firing at him once, though my wing blocked him out most of the time, me being on the inside of the circle. I finally noted the Fw 190 stalling and knew that we would get him eventually. We were right on the treetops and he was afraid of spinning. I wasn't as the P-51 is an honest aeroplane.

'After about two more circles he started stalling, and he was firing his guns as he crashed through a small grove of trees. He emerged on the other side a flaming ball of wreckage. As Lt Harris observed strikes from his burst at this aeroplane, I am sharing it with him.'

Capt Jack Warren was flying wing to 364th CO Maj Dregne when they spotted a pair of Fw 190Ds, which split-ess'ed on sighting the P-51s. Warren reported;

'They pulled out at about 10,000 ft and Maj Dregne made a pass at one and I got a head-on shot at the other as he kicked into a violent spiral and then spun down to a lower altitude. Maj Dregne overshot the first '190, and our No 3 man, Lt James Strode, made several passes. Each time the enemy aircraft would loop with a full roll on top.'

After the third loop the Fw 190 got onto Strode's tail and Strode broke. 'I came in on the enemy aircraft and he then headed for the deck', Warren said. 'I closed to about 300 yards and gave him a long burst. He again looped and rolled, and this time on the top of the loop in a roll he fired at Maj Dregne, who was covering me. I followed, rolled out and came in again. He dove for the deck again, flying between trees, houses and under power lines. I closed to about 300 yards and fired a long burst, this time with only one gun firing. I noted smoke pouring out as he got lower and lower and I passed over him. He crashed in a field about 50 miles southeast of Berlin. Both Maj Dregne and Lt Strode saw the aeroplane crash, and all three of us will admit that the long-nose '190 is fast and manoeuvrable, and this pilot was way above average.'

On the way home Lt Col Graham joined the three-aircraft White Flight, comprising the 362nd FS's Lt John England and Capt 'Bud' Anderson and Lt Edward Simpson from the 363rd FS – England and Anderson would subsequently become the group's second and third ranking aces, respectively. As they made their way west, three Bf 109s crossed in front of them, apparently intent on downing a straggling Flying Fortress. Missouri-born Anderson reported;

'We bounced them. One broke up and one broke down and one proceeded to attack the bomber with a P-51 (flown by Lt John England) on his tail. I came in from behind and underneath, closing to 50 yards, and commenced firing. A big piece of the left wing flew off the Me 109 and it split-ess'ed, then rolled into a slow spiral toward the ground.'

Anderson then went after another fighter;

'I fired two short bursts at a large angle, pulling my nose ahead of him until I couldn't see him, trying to make him break. After the second try, I looked across the circle and saw white smoke pouring from his radiators. The canopy came off and he bailed out at about 5000 ft. The enemy aircraft went straight in and exploded.'

England had been just behind Anderson, and when the latter straightened out and saw this his heart sank because he thought England had bagged the Bf 109. After he landed Anderson was trudging over to the intelligence office, ready to confirm England's kill, when the latter bounded up to him. Before Anderson could offer his congratulations, England shouted 'What a shot! That was the best piece of shooting I've ever seen'. Anderson all but skipped to the intelligence office to make his very first claim. Lt Col Graham and Maj Hayes also scored victories during the mission.

A period of bad weather and the grounding of the Mustang fleet due to defective engine mounting bolts delayed the next mission until 16 March, when P-51s escorted bombers to Munich. Near Ulm, Capt Glen Davis was flying with the second element in the 364th FS's Blue Flight, having lost his wingman in an earlier run-in with German fighters in which he had shared in the destruction of a Bf 110 with Lt Richard Peterson. The three Mustangs were climbing back through the clouds when five Bf 109s came down through a break in the overcast, but their pilots failed to spot the P-51s. Davis reported;

'We let them get below us then bounced them from above. I singled out the last one and he went for the deck. While he was looking back at me he touched the snow but pulled it back and kept on going. I gave him a burst from 300 yards, observing strikes, and he cut his engine and began a glide for an open snow-covered field. I closed on him, firing steadily all the way, observing my bullets completely riddle his aeroplane. Just as I pulled up to avoid collision, he exploded. Pieces of his aeroplane hit the top and leading edge of my right wing, smashing it flat. I climbed back up to 29,000 ft and came home alone. I can truthfully say that I owe my life to the excellence of American materials and workmanship.'

Capt Glendon Davis' P-51B-5 Mustang 43-6878 *Pregnant Polecat* displays an impressive scoreboard – eight swastikas (representing his 7.5 kills) and an assortment of symbols denoting bombing missions and two fighter sweeps. The significance of the two small bombs among the larger markings is unknown. This aircraft suffered engine failure over France on 28 April 1944, forcing Davis to take to his parachute. He avoided capture and eventually returned to the UK *(Olmsted via Roeder)*

A rare photograph of Lt Fletcher Adams' P-51B-1 43-12468 *Southern Belle* taxiing out for a mission in March 1944. Adams became an ace before he was shot down in this aircraft by a Bf 109 on 30 May. He was taken prisoner but murdered by his captors (*Olmsted via Roeder*)

This victory, along with the shared Bf 110, took Glen Davis' tally to 5.5 victories, thus giving the 364th FS pilot the distinction of being the first pilot in the 357th FG to 'make ace'. Squadronmate Capt Jack Warren would emulate his achievement a short while later.

While Blue, White and Green flights were tangling with the Germans below the bombers, Red Flight, led by Maj Hayes, was above them. Soon, according to Hayes, 'three or maybe four twin-engined enemy aircraft made a sorry attack on a tight formation of three boxes of B-17s. I called the flight to attack, and while going down they all broke up. One headed south, which I closed on, with my wingman as cover. At 300 yards my first burst had not enough lead. Still closing, my second burst caught him square and started a fire in the left engine. He reacted by straightening out, whereupon he caught the full effect of all my guns. This was at about 50-100 yards, and I observed his canopy, in addition to other debris, leave the aeroplane. I went under him and noticed both engines burning. I broke away to come back again when I saw one parachute open and the aircraft go straight down, where it exploded in a snow field.'

Capt Jack Warren spotted a single Fw 190 flying straight and level at 1000 ft and 'closed in to about 100 yards from astern and fired a short burst. I observed numerous strikes on and around the cockpit. The enemy aircraft started a spiral to the left and crashed in an orchard. The pilot undoubtedly was killed'. Warren later intercepted some Bf 110s near Augsburg, shooting two of them down to raise his score to five. He had become the 357th FG's second ace.

Meanwhile, Deputy Group Leader and ex-362nd FS CO Lt Col Hubert Egenes spotted an enemy aircraft 5000 ft below him. A veteran of the 17th PS in Java (where, serving alongside Maj Hayes, he had claimed a single aerial victory), Egenes dived and opened fire from 250 yards. Sending the fighter spinning down in flames, he duly reported;

'Upon pulling up from this encounter I noticed a Me 109 forming on another '109's wing. The first pilot was rocking his wings, apparently signalling for both of us to join up. They must have thought I was friendly, for they allowed me to fly up by the No 2 man. We were all in a gentle climb straight ahead. Then I pulled up directly behind the wingman and started firing. Pieces flew off his aeroplane and it began burning. He went out of control, rolled over on his back and went down.'

Two P-51s and their pilots were lost but the group downed 13, with future aces Maj Irwin Dregne and Lt William Reese claiming their first victories – Reese was credited with two kills.

Capt Jack Warren had little time to enjoy his status as an ace, however. Flying with Lt Edwin Sutton off Ostend on 18 March, the weather deteriorated and Warren told Sutton to pull in close and stay in formation. Several minutes later the latter glanced at his instruments and realised something was wrong. 'My airspeed was about 300 mph and I was in a turn to the left', reported Sutton. 'I saw Capt Warren's aeroplane below me and to the left. He was inverted. That was the last time I saw Capt Warren's ship'. Warren was listed as missing in action. Sutton was himself lost diving vertically into cloud 11 days later.

During that same mission, future nine-kill ace Lt Fletcher Adams from Ida, Louisiana, was escorting a straggling B-17 back from Augsburg when he spotted two Bf 109s almost immediately ahead of him;

Lt John Carder's P-51B-15 42-106777 *Taxpayer's Delight* shows evidence of the pilot's success against the Luftwaffe. Carder joined the ranks of the aces on 11 April 1944 over Hanover (*Olmsted via Roeder*)

'An instant later they noticed me and went down. I followed them to the deck and closed on one of them to about 250 yards. I gave the enemy aircraft a burst as he pulled up and observed strikes on his wings and fuselage. Then he hit the ground and a big ball of fire shot upwards. The ship bounced into the air, hit the ground again and exploded.'

Lt Richard Peterson also added a Bf 109 kill to his growing tally.

GOOD LUCK, BAD LUCK

During a mission to Bordeaux on 26 March, the 363rd FS's Lt William Overstreet had his oxygen hose cut by a flak fragment. He passed out but came to 90 minutes later with his aircraft in a spin and a dead engine! He quickly switched fuel tanks, re-started the engine and pulled out at treetop level. He returned to Leiston with his tanks all but dry.

The group's run of variable luck continued during an escort to Dijon on 28 March. The 362nd's lead flight found an airfield crowded with aircraft and dived to attack, Lt Rod Starkey reporting, 'We had just entered the field when Lt Col Egenes made a very sharp turn to his right in front of me. I slid over to get out of the way. Then I commenced firing at a Ju 88 on the ground'. When Starkey glanced back, he saw Egenes' aircraft hit the extreme right-hand side of the airfield. 'I saw this ball of fire and pieces of an aeroplane flying about'. Egenes, whose P-51B had been hit by light flak, perished in the crash.

The group destroyed five Ju 88s and set fire to a hangar but it was a poor exchange for the loss of such an experienced fighter pilot. On 29 March the group lost three more pilots, two from the 363rd FS in a collision and one from the 364th FS to a probable oxygen system failure. The day's only victory was claimed by 362nd FS CO, and future eight-kill ace, Capt Joe Broadhead when he downed a Bf 109 over Brunswick.

Poor weather kept the group grounded until 8 April, when Maj Hayes led an escort to Brunswick once again. Six German fighters fell to the group's guns, with future aces Lts Don Bochkay, Leonard 'Kit' Carson and John Pugh among the victors. The Luftwaffe was back up to challenge the 357th three days later when, just after rendezvousing with bombers headed for Sorau, the 364th's Green Flight encountered a single Bf 109 which dived for cover. Lt Carder reported;

'After approximately five minutes of chasing, firing numerous bursts and observing numerous strikes, I shot the engine out of the Bf 109. The enemy pilot tried to crash land at a speed in excess of 200 mph. The enemy aircraft hit the ground, bounced over high wires and a road and crashed into the ground and exploded.'

This victory took John Carder's tally to five, thus making him the 357th FG's third ace. Like Capt Warren, he too was from the 364th FS.

A short while later, Lt Fletcher Adams, who had been with the bombers for about 20 minutes, spotted a trio of Bf 109s below him. His flight leader, Lt John England, took the tail-end fighter and Adams took the second Messerschmitt in the formation. Both men chased their quarry to the deck, Adams reporting;

'The enemy aeroplane took evasive action, turning and skidding. I fired several bursts when he was going in and out of the clouds. A light stream of black smoke came out of the aeroplane and he went into a cloud. I went over the cloud and next saw the pilot in a parachute. I saw an aeroplane behind me, which I assumed to be my wingman. When I turned, however, he began to shoot at me from about 500 yards. I went down in evasive action to about 20 ft and pulled up sharply to the right. The enemy aeroplane tried to follow this manoeuvre. After I had nearly completed a 360-degree turn, I saw the enemy aeroplane spin into the ground, explode and burn. I saw no parachute this time.'

The 363rd FS's White Flight, meanwhile, had sighted an He 111 'sneaking along right on the ground', according to 'Bud' Anderson. 'The first pass wasn't so good. I pulled up and the rest of the flight came in'. After Lt Henry Kayser fired a burst into the cockpit and Lt William Overstreet shot it up from dead astern, Anderson 'stitched' the He 111's fuselage from tail to cockpit. Then Lt Edward Simpson came in and set the left engine ablaze. 'He tried to crash land, and did', said Simpson. 'The ship burst into flames after hitting a pole and sliding along the ground. The crew jumped out.'

Simpson, Kayser and Anderson each added individual victories during the mission as well. In all, the group destroyed 25 enemy aircraft. The victors included future aces Lts Gilbert O'Brien, John Pugh, Arval Roberson, Charles Peters, Richard Peterson, William Reese, LeRoy Ruder and Robert Shaw, each of whom downed one enemy aircraft. Half-credits were awarded to Lts John England and Don Bochkay.

On 13 April, as the 357th was heading home from Lucheld, Lt John England spotted Lt Leonard 'Kit' Carson attacking an Fw 190 near Mannheim and he went to investigate. England subsequently reported;

Lt John Carder's *Taxpayer's Delight* displays six of his seven victories – a tally he scored between 22 February and 24 April 1944. He was shot down in this aircraft by enemy fighters near Schweinfurt on 12 May and became a PoW. Carder, who saw further action in the Korean War, perished in a flying accident in the US on 1 October 1961 *(Olmsted via Roeder)*

'As we were heading down I saw two Fw 190s about 1000 ft below me. I started after them. They saw me and dived. I pulled up to within 150 yards and fired a short burst at one of them at around 10,000 ft. At 5000 ft we were still going straight down. I gave him another short burst from about 140 yards, observing smoke coming out of the enemy aircraft. After the Fw 190 began a gradual pull-out, the pilot bailed out, going better than 450 mph.'

In addition to the kills achieved by Carson and England, five more enemy fighters were shot down. Budding aces Capt Glen Davis and Lts Robert Becker and Robert Shaw each scored one victory.

During an escort mission to Eschwege on the 19th, just after the lead box of bombers had hit the target, the Luftwaffe struck another box further back in the stream. 'We made a 180-degree turn and found this box under attack by approximately 20 Fw 190s and Me 109s', Capt Davis explained, 'with other P-51s engaging them. I saw two Fw 190s shoot down a B-17 and then get on the tail of a lone red-nosed P-51'. As Davis led the flight down, Lt Morris Stanley spotted two Fw 190s making an attack on his leader from 'nine o'clock'. He reported;

'I turned into the two Fw 190s and they started a steep turn to the left. I fired across the noses of both, and the '190 on the right started a fast roll to the right. He stalled, half-snapped to the right, hit the trees and then the ground, at which point he exploded.'

Unaware of the action behind him, Davis chased the two Fw 190s menacing the Mustang;

'We caught them at about 5000 ft and I got in a good burst at one of them, seeing strikes all over him. They chased the lone P-51 down to the deck, where we got them off his tail. I got a short head-on burst on my man as he was trying to get onto the tail of my wingman, Lt Thomas Harris. I immediately reversed my turn to find the two '190s straightened out. I called to Lt Harris to take the left and I would take the right. Just as I was getting into firing position, my Fw 190 made a perfect peel-off and went straight into the ground from 50 ft, exploding and burning.'

Harris finished off his Fw 190 as well.

The lead flight of the 364th FS, led by Maj Tommy Hayes, also turned and went after the fighters. Hayes later reported;

'I found seven Me 109s lined up abreast for a tail attack from below. I was unable to prevent an attack where one B-17 caught fire, but I did drive off a subsequent attack. We chased them, and after several turns they headed for the deck from 23,000 ft. The seven split into four and then three. At 15,000 ft the four I was pursuing at 700 to 800 yards split, with three going off to the right. My sights set on the one going straight, and I continued after him. At 250 yards my bursts cut his entire tail assembly away.'

Tommy Hayes had just become an ace. John Carder also scored a kill, and a sweep in the Bremen area on 22 April netted single victories

Lt Don Bochkay's second Mustang was well-known P-51B-5 43-6963 *SPEEDBALL ALICE*. His first aircraft was short-lived P-51C-1 42-103041 *Alice in Wonderland*, which was shot down by a Bf 109 over Hanover on 8 March 1944. Its pilot, Lt William W Gambill, bailed out and was made a PoW but he was later killed during an Allied bombing raid. Bochkay scored 7.833 victories while flying B/C-model Mustangs, before transitioning to the P-51D in late July 1944 (*Olmsted via Roeder*)

The 357th FG's first ace, Capt Glen Davis had scored 7.5 victories by the time he suffered an engine failure in *Pregnant Polecat* and was forced to bail out over France on 28 April 1944. The French underground rescued him, transporting him to Paris a week after it was liberated. Like most successful USAAF evaders, Davis was sent home to avoid the risk of his being shot down again and revealing details of Resistance operations to the Germans (*Olmsted via Roeder*)

for future 362nd FS aces Capt Joe Broadhead and Lt Gilbert O'Brien.

During the 24 April mission to Erding, the 363rd's Blue Flight, with Capt 'Bud' Anderson leading, was about ten miles north of Augsburg when several Bf 109s started a run on them from above. Lt Jim Browning's flight went after the fighters, but in the process Lt Ralph Donnell collided with a Bf 110 and he became a PoW. The Bf 110s then entered a defensive Lufbery Circle and a second 357th pilot, Lt Frank Conaghan of the 362nd, collided with a *Zerstörer* and was killed.

Meanwhile, six Bf 109s made the mistake of passing immediately below the 363rd's Red Flight. 'We dropped our tanks and Capt Montgomery Throop dove to attack the last enemy aircraft as it went under us', recalled Lt Don Bochkay. 'I pulled up to cover the first element. As Capt Throop was shooting, the lead enemy aircraft broke hard to the left, made a 360-degree turn and came out on Lt Throop's wingman. I dove down, closing in to about 250 yards. I gave him a short burst and hits were seen around the tail and right wing. The enemy aircraft then went into a violent slip to the right. I gave him another burst, hitting him just in front of the tail assembly. His whole tail broke off, making his aeroplane tumble in.'

The enemy pilot was forced to take to his parachute. A second Bf 109 started a climb after making a pass on a flight of Mustangs, 'pulling streamers from the wings nearly all the time', according to Lt Carder. 'I closed to 250 yards and fired three long bursts, causing the enemy aircraft to emit dense smoke. The pilot bailed out at 7000 ft. I believe he was hit as he jumped'. This proved to be Carder's seventh, and last, kill.

The group had downed 22 enemy aircraft in total. The victors included Fletcher Adams and John England, who accounted for three Bf 110s apiece to make them aces, Lt Joseph Pierce, who downed two, and future aces Capt Ed Hiro and Lts Jim Browning, Richard Peterson and William Reese, who each claimed one. In exchange, the group had lost no fewer than four Mustangs, with one pilot killed and three captured.

A bomber escort mission on 28 April was notable only for the loss of 7.5-victory ace Capt Glen Davis, who suffered an engine failure in his P-51B west of Alford, in France – the target of that day's *Ramrod*. The native of Parma, Idaho, succeeded in evading capture and was eventually returned to the UK seven months later, although he did not return to frontline flying.

Two days later, while heading back to Leiston, the pilots of the 363rd sighted a box of bombers under attack by a swarm of German fighters. 'Six Fw 190s came through my section head-on', reported 'Bud' Anderson. 'Two broke down and the others turned right. By using 20 degrees of flaps and full throttle, I pulled around on their tails in one turn and started firing. It must've scared the hell out of them as they all hit the deck. I then picked out two together and followed, attacking the last man and getting in three good bursts. I had to pull up as I was overrunning him. He straightened out and ran. I then rolled back and followed. As I closed in again, a blue-nosed P-51 came in very steep and fast in front of me. He pulled up and out, the Fw 190 pulled up and the pilot bailed out and the ship crashed. I don't even know if the "blue noser" even fired.'

Anderson's victory was one of nine attributed to the group that day. Other kills were credited to Capt Joe Broadhead and Lts Robert Becker and Gilbert O'Brien, while Lts Joseph Pierce and Richard Peterson downed two to become aces.

Both Anderson and Pierce again claimed victories on 8 May when the 363rd FS encountered Fw 190s near Soltau whilst escorting bombers attacking Berlin. The ensuing battle ended in a draw, with two Mustangs lost (purportedly to flak) and single German fighters falling to the guns of 'Bud' Anderson and Joe Pierce.

Four days later, while escorting 'big friends' to Brux, Lt William Reese was flying on Capt Carder's wing when he spotted two Bf 109s coming in on his leader's tail. 'I called Carder to break right', recalled Reese. 'We then came around on the tail of the enemy aircraft. I followed it from 8000 ft to the deck, firing short bursts at 400 yards, but I was unable to close. Finally, after a ten-minute chase, I observed strikes on the enemy aircraft's engine and it began to smoke. I then closed to within 100 yards and observed strikes all over the German fighter. At this time Capt Carder passed over me from my right to the left and this was the last I saw of him.'

The engine in Carder's P-51B had been hit in the initial pass by the Bf 109s, forcing him to crashland northwest of Schweinfurt. The seven-victory ace quickly became a PoW. In exchange, the group accounted for 14 enemy aircraft, with single Fw 190s and Bf 109s falling to present/future aces Maj Dregne, Capts 'Bud' Anderson and William O'Brien and Lts Joe Pierce and William Reese – both Anderson and Reese actually 'made ace' with these claims. Capts John Storch, Richard Peterson and Fletcher Adams and Lt Arval Roberson, all of whom were either aces already or destined for 'acedom', made shared victory claims.

Col Graham led a 13 May escort mission to Posen and the end result was six enemy aircraft shot down for no cost to the group. Ace Capt Richard Peterson was credited with 1.5 Me 410s destroyed and future ace Lt Robert Shaw also shared in the destruction of a Messerschmitt twin-engined bomber destroyer.

Six days later the group was back over Berlin. The 363rd's Blue Flight had just made a rendezvous with the bombers when pilots sighted approximately 100 German fighters heading for their charges. Lt Charles Peters reported;

'Part of the squadron went for the main bunch but I saw three slightly higher than I was, so I climbed after them in a Lufbery. I was out-turning and out-climbing them up to 31,000 ft. I fired at the last man and saw a strike on his canopy. The ship rolled over and went straight down. I continued turning with the other two until the last man broke away to the left and I followed him down to 12,000 ft. He finally levelled out and

I got in a good burst, with strikes at the wing roots. He broke hard to the left and then blew up. The pilot was thrown out and his 'chute opened.'

Lt Robert Foy, a hard-charger from Oswego, New York, destroyed one Bf 109 for his first kill, then closed in on two more. When the pilots of these aircraft spotted him, they 'immediately pulled into a sharp turn to the left', Foy reported. 'The lead ship of this two-ship formation collided with the outside '109 attempting a head-on pass. The wing of this ship struck squarely in the propeller of the other and was shorn off at the fuselage. The ship burst into flames and I saw no 'chute. The other enemy aircraft lost its prop and the engine nacelle seemed to be crushed, and the '109 started into what might be described as an irregular spin.'

Foy, who was credited with three Bf 109s destroyed, would eventually finish his combat tour with 15 victories.

Maj Irwin Dregne was leading the 364th when he spotted the same huge formation of German fighters, but they scattered before he could reach them;

'I started after a Me 109 and he split-ess'ed for the deck. I dove after him. At about 14,000 ft the Me 109 was in a vertical dive and started rolling. He went into a tight spiral and then started spinning. I followed him down waiting for him to recover. At 5000 ft his canopy came off and I saw the pilot jump. I saw the aeroplane crash but I never saw the parachute open. I was never closer than 1000 yards to the Me 109, and didn't fire my guns.'

Future ace Capt John Storch picked out a straggler, which dived for safety. He reported;

'I followed him and he began to take evasive action, skidding and slipping and half-rolling. When he reached about 13,000 ft he suddenly began to spin. I followed him down and pulled out of my dive when I could see from the way he was spinning that he would be unable to recover. I watched the Bf 109 spin into the ground and explode. I did not observe any 'chute. From the way in which the enemy aircraft was spinning I believe the pilot must have in some way damaged his aeroplane by taking such violent evasive action at excessive speeds, as we were both probably indicating about 500 mph.'

Meanwhile, future ace Lt LeRoy Ruder spotted more German fighters at a higher altitude than the first large group that the 357th had engaged as they went for the bombers. He recalled;

'After a few minutes I was in position to fire on an Fw 190. I closed to about 300 yards and opened fire, observing numerous strikes on the fuselage and wings. The enemy aircraft completed a couple of rolls and tight turns. Finally, he straightened out long enough for me to fire a few more bursts from about 250 yards. At the time we were going at a great speed, with my aircraft nearly out of control. As I fired my last burst, the enemy aircraft started into another roll, with pieces flying from it. Suddenly, the enemy aircraft fell apart. Large sections of the fuselage and tail assembly ripped off and the enemy aircraft tumbled toward the ground, end over end. I broke off my attack at 10,000 ft and climbed back up to locate my flight.'

Additional victories were claimed by aces Capts Fletcher Adams and Ed Hiro and by Lt Arval Roberson. In all, the group scored ten kills for no losses.

On 21 May the group conducted a series of strafing attacks over northern Germany that saw pilots claim 12 aircraft destroyed. These successes came at a high price, however, as two aces were lost to flak. Lts William C Reese and Joseph F Pierce were both killed, the former crashing near Stralsund and the latter coming down near Anklam. Pierce was from the 363rd FS, and a second pilot from the unit was also lost just minutes after his demise. The fighter of 364th FS pilot Lt John Howell was struck by flak too, although he managed to make it home. Once back at Leiston, he recalled Lt Reese's demise;

'We went down to the deck and headed north from Berlin, spotting a train which appeared to be in a marshalling yard. We were in a spread formation and had just started the strafing run when I smelled a rat and called "Flak train! Let's get out of here". About the same instant Bill Reese got hit and went into the water immediately, just off shore from the town of Stralsund. At the same time my aeroplane was hit, and was responding poorly to the controls. While looking for an area to crashland, I got the bird under control with throttle and trim tab and headed for home. The old Mustang stayed together, and it was throttle and trim tab all the way home.

'Losing Bill Reese was a severe blow. He was a fine person, outstanding pilot and true friend.'

Three days later the group flew two missions, and a single kill was claimed by future ace Capt William O'Brien east of Berlin.

During an escort mission to Ludwigshafen on the 27th, the 364th jumped a large formation of Bf 109s about 20 miles southwest of Strasbourg. 'I was leading Blue Flight, with Lt Thomas Harris flying my No 3, when we went down on a Me 109 that was diving away', recalled Maj John Storch. 'Lt Harris' element was in position when we went down, followed by our Green Flight'.

Lt John Howell's P-51B-10 42-106447 *SHOO SHOO BABY* carried the pilot home after an encounter with German flak on 21 May 1944 – a mission during which his wingman, ace Lt William Reese, was shot down and killed. *SHOO SHOO BABY* sustained damage to its tail. The aircraft was repaired and took to the skies again fitted with a blown Malcolm canopy. Having survived for more than a year with the 364th FS, 42-106447 was lost in a mid-air collision with P-51B 43-24766 during a training mission on 27 February 1945 that cost the lives of rookie pilots Lts Ralph E Eisert and Robert R Hoffman. Neither man had flown a mission prior to their deaths (*USAF*)

Capt John England's camera-gun captured this shot of a Luftwaffe pilot leaping from his Bf 109 north of Strasbourg following the ace's attack on 27 May 1944 (*Olmsted via Roeder*)

Lt LeRoy A Ruder was the No 3 man in Green Flight, and he reported;

'As my flight leader was getting into position to fire on one of the enemy aircraft, I observed a Me 109 trying to get into position to attack him. I immediately broke into the enemy aircraft and at the same time expected my wingman, Lt Cyril Conklin, to break with me. I do not know where he went. I had my hands full with the '109 I was fighting and, since my radio was out, could not ask my wingman for his position.'

Conklin scored two kills during the battle but fell victim to a Bf 109 and ended up a PoW. Storch noted;

'When the dogfight was finished I had my No 2 and Green Flight's Nos 1 and 2 and a 352nd FG aeroplane with me. I started spiralling for altitude and the bombers, which were by now out of sight. I called Lt Harris and finally got him, and he said he was okay and hunting for me. I told him my position as nearly as possible, my altitude and my course, and I stayed in the area for approximately 15 minutes.'

Harris, who had just 'made ace' by downing a pair of Bf 109s, never made the rendezvous as he almost certainly collided with squadronmate Lt Dean Post. The latter was killed, but Harris managed to bail out into captivity. Despite these losses, the 364th had made the enemy pay by claiming an impressive 12.5 victories. Again, the aces predominated the scoring, with Storch responsible for 2.5 kills and Harris and Lt Morris Stanley two each – these successes also gave Stanley ace status. LeRoy Ruder and Robert Shaw each got one.

During the same mission, the 362nd was climbing behind the lead box of bombers when 'between five and six enemy aircraft came down through the bombers and turned left onto the same heading that we had', recalled ace Lt Fletcher Adams. He reported;

'We started to chase them. An Me 109 went to the left, with Capt England following, and I saw pieces fall off that aircraft as he shot at him. The second one went to the right with Capt Calvert Williams shooting at him. There were pieces coming off him too. The two Fw 190s directly in front of us started a gentle turn to the left. The one on the inside tightened his turn and I told Lt Gilbert O'Brien to get him.'

The Fw 190 made two 360-degree turns, with O'Brien on its tail;

'I took a 90-degree deflection shot. Not seeing any hits, he rolled out square in front of me. I had a little excess speed and came right in behind him. I began to overshoot and saw his canopy come off. I slid right up beside him with my flaps down. He bailed out as I was alongside him

27

at about 12,000 ft. The pilot's chest was covered in blood and he hit the rudder. I did not see his 'chute open.'

The demise of this Fw 190 boosted Gilbert O'Brien's tally to exactly five kills. Meanwhile, the second Fw 190 continued in a gentle turn, with Adams in pursuit. The latter fired, scoring hits;

'At about 10,000 ft he seemed to be trying an outside loop, so I rolled out, and when I lifted my wing I saw an explosion on the ground and a parachute in the vicinity of the crash'.

In addition to these victories three more pilots scored singles, including aces Capt John England and Lt John Pugh.

The 363rd FS was in on the action too. Capt William O'Brien was leading, and he ordered White Flight to attack a gaggle of Bf 109s, with Blue and Green Flights giving cover. Capt 'Bud' Anderson headed up White Flight, and as they raced for the front of the formation, 'my No 3 called in four bandits coming in on us at "four o'clock"' he confirmed. 'We broke into them and they pulled up and circled, trying to get at us. With full throttle and RPM, I was able to close around and climb on them. They all straightened out and tried to run, while their No 4 climbed up – my No 3, Lt Edward Simpson, went after him while I chased the other three.'

Simpson caught his quarry at 30,000 ft, and after hitting him with two bursts he saw the pilot bail out. Meanwhile, Anderson pursued the other three fighters;

'I closed slowly on No 3 and waited until I was in close, and dead astern, then fired a good burst, getting hits all over. Smoke streamed and his canopy may have come off. He rolled over and went down out of control. I singled out No 2. He dove and pulled up in a left climbing turn. I pulled inside and overshot – he straightened out and I pulled up, watching him as he tried to get on my No 2's tail. He stalled and I went after him. He repeated with another left climbing turn. I overshot again and the same thing followed. The third time I made up my mind I wouldn't lose him, so as he pulled up I fired. The first tracers went over his right wing. I skidded my nose over and strikes appeared all over. I slid alongside and saw fire break out. The Me 109 rolled over slowly and went straight in from 28,000 ft.'

O'Brien, meanwhile, had spotted a Bf 109 chasing a P-51. He fired a 90-degree deflection shot to persuade the German pilot to break off his attack, before manoeuvring behind the enemy fighter. After several rounds had struck it near the cockpit, smoke began to billow from the Messerschmitt and the pilot bailed out.

Future seven-kill ace Capt Jim Browning was leading Green Flight, and he later reported;

'I saw two Me 109s going in the opposite direction. I turned and gave one a shot with deflection. I don't think I hit him. He then pulled almost straight up. I climbed with him and waited until I was about 250 yards away and I levelled out. I then gave him a long burst. I got hits and coolant came out. He then turned and I overshot him. I made a circle and came back at him. He was in a slight dive, with coolant still coming out. I gave him another long burst from about 20 degrees deflection. I could see him bowed over in the cockpit, as if trying to fasten his 'chute. The last burst I gave him was directly into the cockpit and the right side of his aeroplane. He bailed out and I pulled up over him.'

Posing for the camera at Leiston on 28 May 1944, 357th FG HQ pilot and former CO of the 364th FS Maj 'Tommy' Hayes is seen with his groundcrew and his first *Frenesi* (a P-51B whose serial remains unknown) after he had destroyed a Bf 109 over Magdeburg *(USAF)*

According to Browning's wingman, the German pilot's parachute opened but he fell out of the harness and plummeted to earth.

During the next day's mission to Magdeburg, the group had just rendezvoused with the bombers when the American force was engaged by more than 100 German fighters that ripped head-on through the bombers in line-abreast formations. Maj Joe Broadhead subsequently reported;

'After the first wave passed, I peeled off and started following. A solitary Fw 190 also peeled off, leaving the formation. He was unaware that I was following him, so I held my fire until I had closed to within 200 yards. I took careful aim and gave him one long burst, hitting him in the tail, fuselage and wings. Smoke immediately started coming from him and he did a roll to start a split-s and I overshot him. As I crossed him, I saw a fire starting from his belly.'

Flying above the bombers, the 362nd had seen German fighters make three passes at the 'heavies', which held position nevertheless. Then, 'about 500 yards to the left of my flight, an Fw 190 was making an attack on a P-51', recalled future 18.5-kill ace Lt 'Kit' Carson;

'I broke from my flight to attack the Fw 190 and he broke off his attack and dove for the deck. I fired several times during the dive but we were going so fast that I couldn't get an accurate shot. He levelled out at about 500 ft above the ground, chopped his throttle, dropped flaps and made a steep turn to the right. I overshot, but came back and we got into a Lufbery. I fired several times from 250-500 yards at 140 mph. I saw several strikes on his fuselage and wings. He levelled off and started to glide towards the ground, his engine burning. About 20 ft off the ground he jettisoned his canopy. His ship went into a slight bank to the left, hit the ground, cartwheeled and burst into flames.'

The 364th was at the rear of the formation and could do nothing to stop the initial attacks, but its pilots caught the Bf 109s as they passed through the bombers. Lt Col Tommy Hayes was leading the squadron, and he reported;

'I was able to get onto the tail of one of the Me 109s, which now began to dive. I fired three short bursts. After the first strikes he skidded, I suppose to look back. I fired again, seeing debris and the canopy come off. Just as the third burst was fired it looked like the pilot had started

Capt Fletcher Adams of the 362nd FS was one of the 357th FG's leading aces when he was shot down by a Bf 109 west of Bernburg on 30 May 1944. Although he succeeded in bailing out of his Mustang, Adams was murdered by his captors (*Olmsted via Roeder*)

to get out. However, at that instant the ship actually disintegrated. I picked up my element leader, Lt John Howell, and covered him as he nailed a Me 109 too, its pilot taking to his parachute.'

Eight victories fell to the group with no losses, with aces Lts LeRoy Ruder and Charles Peters and Capt Richard Peterson also being successful.

On 30 May, during an escort mission to Bernburg the 362nd caught the bombers just in time to disrupt an attack by a force of 75 Bf 109s, Fw 190s, Bf 110s and Me 410s. 'Kit' Carson found himself looking down on an Me 410 'that was jockeying for position to attack. He immediately went into a dive and my wingman and I followed. I closed to about 250 yards and fired a burst, observing hits on the rudder and right wing. He cut his throttle and I overshot, his gunner firing as I pulled off to the left. I dropped flaps and turned back behind him. By the time I was within range again we were on the deck. I fired another burst and he brushed the tops of some trees and was skipping on a ploughed field. He pulled up, made a left turn over a grove of trees, dished out of the turn and crashed at the edge of the grove.'

Both Capt Robert Becker and Lt Robby Roberson from the 362nd achieved 'acedom' during this clash, the former claiming three Bf 109s destroyed and the latter pilot two.

Four Bf 109s from the same large formation bounced Capt Fletcher Adams' flight from behind out of the sun. 'Before I knew what was happening, tracers were going over my wing and into my aeroplane', recalled Lt Gilbert O'Brien. 'I broke straight down, calling for the rest of my flight to follow suit. As I broke, I looked up and got a flashing picture of a Me 109 firing from close range at Capt Adams. I saw him streaming coolant or coolant smoke. Shortly after this Capt Adams rolled over on his back and split-ess'ed.'

The three remaining Mustangs shot down their attackers. Adams, who had already shared in the destruction of an Me 410 with O'Brien to take his tally to nine victories, bailed out safely but was murdered by the head of the local home guard unit, his regional superior and by the chief of police. After the war, the former was convicted by a war crimes tribunal and sentenced to death. This was commuted to 25 years in prison, however. His co-conspirators were never apprehended.

Having seen Adams shot down, Capt William O'Brien and his wingman rolled into a near-vertical dive and set off in pursuit of a group of Bf 109s. Moments later Lt Robert Foy, leader of O'Brien's second

Capt Richard Peterson's first *Hurry Home Honey* was P-51B-5 43-6935, and it is seen here at Leiston displaying ten victory markings in late May 1944. This aircraft was lost on 20 June 1944 when it was hit by flak north of Paris. Pilot Lt Heyward C Spinks successfully evaded (*Olmsted via Roeder*)

Capt 'Bud' Anderson achieved his eighth kill – a Bf 109 – over Schonebeck on 30 May. Here, for the benefit of the camera and his crewchief, he has also rounded up his shared He 111 kill, on 11 April, to make nine *(Author's collection)*

element, radioed him to tell him that his propeller had failed. 'I told Foy that I was busy, but I'd get to him as soon as I could', O'Brien said later. He duly chased the enemy aircraft to the deck and shot down two of them, giving him ace status. Then he began looking for Foy. Soon, however, he heard Capt Richard Peterson on the radio. 'Don't worry, "O'Bee", I've got him'.

Although low on fuel, Peterson reversed course and found Foy, whose aircraft had a big smear of oil down one side of the fuselage caused by a leaking prop seal – a fact Peterson kept from Foy so as to avoid panicking the less experienced pilot. The two crept along at 180 mph, parallel to and five miles north of the bombers as they droned back to England. Peterson then saw a formation of Bf 109s heading for the 'heavies' just below him. He wanted to attack them but realised his fuel was low and that Foy would be a sitting duck. Instead, he rolled as if he were diving on the German fighters. Their pilots saw him and broke. O'Brien completed the roll and formed up with Foy again.

When the pair were over the Channel Peterson made a mayday call and was told by the air-sea rescue service that the rescue launch was heading their way. Before long Foy noticed a rise in temperature and smelled smoke in the cockpit. Peterson tried to calm Foy, who responded, 'To hell with this!' He jettisoned his canopy and bailed out. Foy's parachute blossomed and the Mustang continued towards the water, but exploded before reaching the surface. Peterson could already see the launch approaching, and less than 30 minutes later Foy was on his way home. When Peterson landed at Leiston his engine quit from lack of fuel before he could taxi back to his stand.

During this mission the group had destroyed 18 German fighters. The day's high scorers were Capt Robert Becker with three (making him an ace), Lts Arval Roberson and William O'Brien with two and Lt Gilbert O'Brien with 1.5. Single kills were attributed to ace Capt 'Bud' Anderson and future aces Capt James Browning and Lt Robert Shaw, the latter sharing his Me 410 with Lt John Howell.

OVERHEAD FOR *OVERLORD*

There were no encounters with the enemy during escort missions flown on 31 May and 2 and 3 June, but it was clear that something was in the offing. On 5 June, after a mission to Abbeville, Leiston was closed and all personnel were barred from leaving the airfield. 'I think the invasion is going to start in the morning, for all of our aeroplanes are being painted in black and white stripes for recognition purposes', Capt LeRoy Ruder wrote in his diary. He was right. The next day the group flew eight sweeps and strafing missions in the areas around Paris, Amiens, Rennes and La Suze.

On the morning of the 6th, Ruder was patrolling five miles southeast of Cherbourg when he radioed his second element leader, Lt Mark Stepelton, that his oil pressure was falling and he let down through the clouds. Ruder's aircraft had been hit by light flak at St Michel-en-Greve. Stepelton got on the radio and told the ace to bail out. 'He said that he saw some land and was going to crashland', Stepelton reported. 'I came out of the overcast and circled, but could see no sign of him'. After the war Stepelton wrote, 'He crash-landed and died soon thereafter. The loss of my friend was so shocking because it happened so fast, and it was beyond his ability to avoid'. Two other Mustangs were also lost to flak that day, with one pilot killed and the other evading capture.

7 June proved to be no easier for the group, with four missions flown to Rennes, Morlaix and Tours. Maj John Storch was leading the 364th's Blue Flight hunting road traffic when they approached the small town of Plancoet. Storch turned his flight to avoid it but intense light flak began harassing the Mustangs and Lt John Denesha's aircraft was hit. He was never seen or heard from again.

The group's aces did not draw blood again until the 14th when, during an area patrol, the 364th's Green Flight sighted some long-nosed Fw 190s. One of them fell to the guns of Lt Robert M Shaw, making him an ace. 'I had just shot down the '190 when Lt James Colburn called "break left"' recalled Shaw. His wingman, Colburn, was firing at a second

This rare shot of Capt 'Kit' Carson's P-51D-5 44-13316 *NOOKY BOOKY II* shows the fighter during the few days that it was marked up as *Mildred*. Photographed at Leiston in June 1944 with assistant crew chief Sgt Livingston Blauvelt III posing beside it, the aircraft arrived just after D-Day, so the invasion stripes remained for several weeks. The fighter's nickname was quickly changed, however. Carson flew this machine through to the late autumn, when it was transferred to Lt Ted Conlin to become *Olivia de H*. The Mustang's final fate is unknown (*Olmsted via Roeder*)

Fw 190, which caught fire. 'Another enemy aircraft was on Lt Colburn's tail and got numerous hits in the cockpit area', reported Shaw, who then saw his wingman's aircraft 'spinning in, crashing and exploding'. Colburn was killed in the crash.

The 357th FG returned to more familiar long range bomber escort missions on 20 June when it accompanied 'heavies' to the German town of Ostermoor. Five enemy aircraft were downed, with Maj Storch and Lt Louis Fecher sharing a Bf 109 – Storch's claim was the only one submitted by a would-be ace.

A further nine days passed before the group encountered the Luftwaffe again. 'Bud' Anderson was leading the 363rd, 'riding herd' on the second box of bombers between Brunswick and Magdeburg, when combat began ahead of the squadron. 'We dropped our tanks and had just started to accelerate forward when eight Fw 190s went under me. They crossed in front of the low squadron of bombers and turned left in a formation resembling one of ours, thus mocking the escorts. It looked like a trap, as eight more came down and bounced our second section. The latter turned into them and seemed to be doing okay, so our section went down on the ones below. I picked the leader and gave him a short burst from about 350 yards dead astern, getting quite a few hits. He did a roll to the right and straightened out, skidding violently. The canopy flew off and he snapped over on his back, at which point he bailed out.

'I then saw another one heading for the clouds. He ducked in, but it was thin and I could see him once in a while, so I followed. He came out in a clear spot and I attacked from the rear, closing to 150 yards and getting quite a few hits. The canopy flew off and the pilot started to climb out, but he settled back into the cockpit. I flew alongside and saw fire break out in the cockpit. He slowly rolled over and went straight in from about 8000 ft, making a huge explosion.

'My wingman came alongside and we started to climb back when another Fw 190 came out of the thin overcast 90 degrees to our course, behind us and above. We circled around on his tail, climbing after him. I cut him off, closed in and started firing. I didn't get hits at first, so I slid around dead astern and got a few good hits. He then took his first evasive action, pulling up through the clouds. I followed, firing. He went down through it again. I got some hits in the cockpit area. The Fw 190 then did a violent snap roll to the right followed by a tight spin. Streamers were coming off his wingtips and tail surfaces and he spun right in, exploding. No 'chute came out.'

Blue Flight, with Capt Don Bochkay leading, was flying above Green Flight. Just after the four Mustangs dropped their tanks and started to turn, Bochkay looked up into the sun and spotted 'four Fw 190s coming down on us followed by four Me 109s. They went past us and broke into Green Flight, dead astern'. Green leader on this occasion was future triple ace Capt Robert Foy;

'They fired and passed over the top of my flight, making a turn to cut us off. I called for Blue Flight to break right and I put 20 degrees of flaps down and cut my throttle, manoeuvring to the rear of the enemy aircraft. I pulled up on the tail of the rear Fw 190. I fired at him and observed strikes all over the fuselage and wings, at which time he straightened up and bailed out in level flight.'

At the same time Bochkay lined up the lead Fw 190 and fired, but the German pilot split-ess'ed and fled. Foy saw a Mustang being chased by a Bf 109 'just off at about "three o'clock" to me and low. I pulled up and dived, ending up below his tail. I followed him for about 15 seconds in close trail. I pulled up and fired two short bursts, observing strikes on his right wing and beneath the fuselage. The Me 109 immediately broke to the left, did one rather fast roll and the pilot bailed out.'

Foy called to his wingman and received no answer. He then radioed his element leader who replied that he had lost Foy when he went after the Bf 109. Foy said;

'I pulled into a sharp left turn and saw a ship on my tail. I pulled into a tighter turn and started to spin into the overcast, recovering after about two turns. I put my flaps down, cut my throttle and continued turning to the left. I had completed about three-fourths of a 360-degree turn when a Me 109 cut across in front of me at high speed. I gave my fighter full throttle, pulling up on his tail. I fired one burst, observing strikes on the right wing. The enemy aircraft did a split-s and I followed him. He pulled out of range in a vertical dive. I glanced at my airspeed, which indicated well over 550 mph. The Me 109 was still pulling away from me, however. I pulled out at 3000 ft and the Me 109 was still in a vertical dive. I climbed up to 6000 ft and circled the immediate area. I did not see the enemy aircraft hit the ground, but there was a spot on the ground that looked as if either a bomb or an aeroplane had gone in.'

Foy's three victories took him to 'acedom'.

Bochkay, in the meantime, had spotted another Bf 109 trying to dive to safety. This time he stuck to his quarry. When he fired, the Messerschmitt's 'ammunition started to explode, tearing bits and pieces from both wings. The pilot then bailed out doing close to 600 mph – he delayed his opening. At 4000 ft the ship caught fire and crashed'. Bochkay was now also an ace.

In all, the group scored 19 victories. In addition to the kills achieved by Anderson, Bochkay and Foy, the group's other 'top guns' also featured prominently among those claiming victories. A single kill was attributed to Capt John Pugh, Lt Col Tommy Hayes claimed 1.5 kills and Capt James Browning scored one and two shared to 'make ace'. Finally, Lt Gerald Tyler downed a Bf 109 for the first of seven kills that he would score over the next four months. In return, the group lost Capt Richard Smith of the 364th FS, who perished when he was shot down by fighters near Leipzig. He had three victories to his name at the time of his demise.

On 1 July the 357th flew an area patrol and downed four fighters, two of which fell to Capt Richard Peterson. Four days later, the group escorted 'heavies' to Béziers. On the way in, Capt Don Bochkay chased two Fw 190s to the deck and scored

Capt Jim Browning shot down an Me 410 and shared in the destruction of another bomber destroyer, as well as an Fw 190, on 29 June 1944 southwest of Leipzig, elevating him to ace status. He is pictured here in the cockpit of his first *GENTLEMAN JIM*, P-51B-5 Mustang 43-6563, which was accidently shot down by another Mustang while strafing near Mortagne, France, on 10 June. Pilot Lt John K Childs was killed (*USAF*)

Capt Richard Peterson's crew admire the ten victory markings displayed by P-51B-5 43-6935 *Hurry Home Honey* sometime after he had become a double ace on the 28 May mission to Magdeburg. Bearing full invasion stripes, the fighter also has a large white cross marking on the fuselage below the kill tally to indicate that the Mustang has been fitted with a fuselage fuel tank (*Olmsted via Roeder*)

'numerous hits around the cockpit' on one of them. 'He went into a spin and spun on in – the pilot didn't get out' reported Bochkay's wingman, Capt Charles Peters. Bochkay was leading his flight back up toward the overcast when he saw two more Focke-Wulf fighters on the deck below him travelling at 180 degrees to his course. He reported later;

'I did a wingover and was closing in for the kill. I was all set to pull the trigger when an Me 109 jumped me from my left. I pulled a feinting break into him and he broke very hard to the right and up. I immediately latched on to the '109, who tried to turn me to the right. I gave him a long burst and saw hits all over him. He began to smoke badly. He then dumped his canopy, so I poured another long burst into him. He flipped over and went straight down. The pilot finally got out, but in doing so he hit the tail.'

Lt Gerald Tyler was flying P-51B-5 43-6376 *LITTLE DUCKFOOT* when he claimed his first two kills, an Fw 190 on 29 June and an Fw 190 on 5 July 1944. Tyler, who hailed from Sarasota, Florida, would become an ace with a triple-kill haul over Maastricht on 19 September 1944 (*Olmsted via Roeder*)

Groundcrewmen help Lt 'Chuck' Yeager strap into his second Mustang, P-51D-5 44-13897 *GLAMOROUS GLEN II*, at Leiston in July 1944. Yeager's flight status was in doubt at this time following his shooting down over France in March 1944 and subsequent evasion back to the UK. This bureaucratic limbo even cost Yeager a kill when he downed a Ju 88 in this aircraft on 5 July before he was cleared to resume combat. Squadronmate Lt Edward Simpson, who was killed in action fighting with the Maquis on 14 August with his score standing at 4.25 victories, was given credit for the Ju 88 (*Olmsted via Roeder*)

Lts Robert Shaw and Gerald Tyler of the 364th FS also claimed single Fw 190 kills to take the group's victory tally for the day to four.

'Chuck' Yeager, meanwhile, had made his way from enemy territory all the way back to London by mid-May. He protested against the usual practice of posting pilots back to the US after evading capture and, while awaiting news of his fate, he was allowed to return to Leiston and fly non-combat missions. On 6 July Yeager and wingman Lt Herschel Pascoe were 'rat racing' when they received a call about a rescue effort near Heligoland. Speeding to the location, they found a Wellington circling a dinghy. Seeing that the rescue attempt was being handled by the RAF, the pair turned for home, but then spotted a low-flying Ju 88. They dived after it and Yeager fired. Pascoe observed strikes on the fuselage.

'The enemy aircraft kept trying to hide in the clouds but he was too low to the water', said Pascoe. 'The second time Yeager fired the enemy aircraft hit the water at high speed and broke into pieces'.

With Yeager's presence in-theatre still in a state of bureaucratic limbo, his name was removed from the mission report and replaced by that of Lt Edward Simpson. Yeager was never given official credit for the kill. A few days later he received word that he could resume flying combat missions with the group once again.

Escorting bombers to Leipzig on 7 July brought more victories. 'Bud' Anderson was leading the 363rd, and he reported later;

'We had been "ess-ing" slowly in front of the bombers for around half-an-hour when I saw three Me 109s at "one o'clock low". I picked the leader and dove down from dead astern. I had a perfect closing speed so I waited until I was about 250 yards away and fired until about 100 yards, getting very good hits. Pieces flew off and his coolant sprayed out, coating my windshield and part of my bubble canopy. The last I saw of the Messerschmitt fighter, he was spinning down, smoking badly.'

Bochkay's Green Flight had been providing top cover, and he saw the Bf 109 crash. The pilot did not escape. The 363rd scored two more kills but lost a Mustang and its pilot during the mission.

There were two escort missions to targets in France on the 14th. During one of them the 364th FS covered Eighth Air Force bombers dropping supplies to French resistance fighters from about 500 ft. Just after the bombers had made their run two Fw 190s attacked them. Capt Mark Stepelton and his wingman, Lt Howard Reed, went after them but 'at the instant we approached the enemy aircraft, ten Me 109s attacked

us', Reed reported. In the resulting melee four German fighters fell, one to Maj Tommy Hayes.

The group resumed scoring during an area patrol to Paris on 25 July. Some P-38s were sighted attacking a marshalling yard, and 'at that moment a gaggle of Fw 190s and Me 109s appeared dead ahead of us', said Lt Ted Conlin. 'I do not think they could have seen us because they rolled over and started an attack on the P-38s. I was flying No 2 on Capt 'Kit' Carson's wing. He rolled over and I followed him down as he tacked on to the rear of an Fw 190'. Meanwhile, the No 3 man in the flight, Capt John Pugh, broke off and latched onto the tail of a Bf 109. He reported:

'He broke to the right and we made a complete turn. We continued to Lufbery down to 5000 ft and I fired several short bursts in a tight turn, with no observed strikes. I continually out-turned him. At about 300 ft above Paris, I closed from 200 ft to about 50 ft, firing all the time. I saw strikes on the canopy, then the pilot bailed out. This enemy aircraft was shot from very close range. It was impossible to miss.'

Pugh became an ace with this success.

Meanwhile, Carson and Conlin continued after the Fw 190. 'At the time, it seemed that we were almost vertical chasing the '190', recalled Conlin. 'The pilot was doing big barrel rolls downward, trying to get us off his tail, but we were right with him. As Capt Carson closed into range he started to get strikes. This, and the ground coming up rather rapidly, caused the German plot to flare out and level off. We were now at approximately 300 ft, and "Kit" was getting hits all over the Fw 190 when the German's engine failed. We were heading east just above the Grand Armée-Champs Elysées Boulevard. It looked like the Fw 190 was going to crash into the Arc de Triomphe! The pilot must have been dead since he did not try to bail out.

'Capt Carson broke away and I was fascinated to watch the prop windmilling as the Fw 190 headed toward its fatal end. All of a sudden I realised that Capt Carson was gone, and there I was at just 300 ft over central Paris, and every soldier with a weapon was firing at me.'

Conlin hugged the Seine for a few miles, literally below the Germans' guns, and made good his escape.

Lt Col Tommy Hayes was at the controls of P-51D-5 44-13318 *Frenesi* when he downed a Bf 109 and shared in the demise of an Me 410 west of Liepzig on 29 June 1944. Hayes' crew was one of the few to maintain the practice of updating mission markings after the tempo of operations increased in the summer of 1944. 44-13318 survived until 15 January 1945, when it was salvaged after suffering damage on 'Big Day' (*Olmsted via Roeder*)

Capt John Pugh sits in the cockpit of his P-51B-10 42-106473 *Geronimo*. He became an ace while flying this aircraft on 25 July 1944 when he shot down a Bf 109 from close range at low altitude over central Paris (*Olmsted via Roeder*)

Deputy CO of the 357th FG Lt Col Irwin Dregne, in P-51D-5 44-13408 *Bobby Jeanne/Aн Fung-Goo II,* and his wingman, possibly Lt Dale Karger (in an unidentified P-51B), prepare for a local flight in September 1944. Dregne's aircraft would eventually be stripped of paint and appear in a natural metal finish. Both pilots would 'make ace' (*Olmsted via Roeder*)

Twenty enemy fighters made the mistake of flying directly in front of the 363rd. 'I picked out what I thought was a Me 109', said Capt Robert Foy. 'He suddenly pulled into a sharp right turn and I put down 20 degrees of flap and followed, giving several bursts. Smoke started pouring out of the right side of the enemy aircraft and he continued turning to the left. I pulled up to avoid colliding with a silver P-51 and then continued on the enemy aircraft's tail. He hit the ground in the middle of a small racetrack.'

Don Bochkay also added one to his score over Paris.

On 29 July the 363rd FS's Red Flight found a large airfield near Merseburg and dropped down to attack it. 'As we did, an Me 109 dove on us slightly to our right', recalled Lt Bill Overstreet. 'I turned into him as soon as I was across the field and he was fairly close. He turned right also, leaving me right behind him. I fired with about 30 degrees deflection and got hits. I closed in, still firing, and hit his coolant. He dropped down right on the ground, and as my wing was in the grass

Lt Bill Overstreet points out the freshly-applied artwork on P-51C-1 42-103309 *BERLIN EXPRESS* while his groundcrew admire their work. Note the whitewall tyres, which was another embellishment provided by the groundcrew (*Olmsted via Roeder*)

Three members of Lt Gilbert O'Brien's groundcrew pose with their aircraft, P-51B-5 43-6787 *SHANTY IRISH*, in August 1944. O'Brien used this fighter to claim most of his seven victories. Two of the ace's successes were shared victories, but they have been marked on the aircraft as full kills. 43-6787 was passed on to Lt James Kenney after O'Brien returned home in August 1944, and it remained in service with the group until February 1945 (*Olmsted via Roeder*)

Fighters from the 362nd FS taxi over the prepared runways at Leiston at the start of the unit's mission to Russia on 6 August 1944. At right is ace Capt Robert Becker's P-51D-10 44-14231 *Sebastian Jr.*, which displays his full scoreboard of seven kills. This aircraft later became Lt Clifford Anderson's *Buddy Boy II* (*Olmsted via Roeder*)

I had to pull up. Pieces of the '109 made holes in my canopy'. Don Bochkay also downed an enemy aircraft over the field.

About 20 miles west of Merseburg the 362nd FS found a large group of Bf 109s trying to organise themselves for an attack. Lt Gilbert O'Brien jumped one and shot it down. Lt Paul E Holmberg 'came in from the left and began firing at the same ship', O'Brien reported. 'Suddenly, his Mustang exploded and disintegrated. There was not the usual flame and smoke when fuel tanks exploded, so I presume that his ammunition box must have been responsible. There is not the slightest chance that he got out alive'.

The 362nd's 'Kit' Carson also added a Bf 109 to his score to give him ace status.

The next day, the group flew a successful sweep of the Paris area. Three enemy aircraft were shot down, including one by future ace Maj Ed Hiro, CO of the 363rd FS.

SHUTTLE ESCORT

On 6 August 64 357th FG Mustangs provided an escort for the fifth shuttle mission to the Soviet Union. Thirty-five members of the ground echelon flew with the 390th Bomb Group (BG) as gunners during its

Another shot of the 362nd FS lining up at Leiston on 6 August 1944. In the foreground is Capt John England in unnamed P-51D-5 Mustang 44-13735. When England swapped this aircraft for his *MISSOURI ARMADA*, it was passed on to Maj Lawrence Giarizzo and became *Toolin' Fool*. It lost a wing while chasing enemy fighters near Naumberg on 2 November 1944, resulting in the death of Giarizzo (*Olmsted via Roeder*)

Mustangs line the airfield at Piryatin folllowing their arrival in the Ukraine during the afternoon of 6 August 1944. Second from the camera is Capt John Pugh's P-51B-10 42-106473 *Geronimo*. He would claim his sixth, and last, kill in this aircraft the following day over Krakow, Poland (*Olmsted via Roeder*)

attack on the Focke-Wulf plant at Rahmel. Nine Fw 190s were spotted just after making landfall, but the German fighters made no move to intercept them. Had they done so the Mustangs would have lacked the fuel to reach Russia.

Intercepting the bombers over Poland, nine Bf 109s from JG 51 went after the 'heavies' but Lt Robert Shaw and his flight cut them off. Shaw peppered one of them, sending it down in flames. Lt 'Bud' Nowlin chased another fighter, which was being flown by Hauptmann Gunther Schack, *Staffelkapitan* of III/JG.51. He fired a burst and Schack split-ess'ed away, with Nowlin in pursuit. Another burst brought a spray of coolant from Schack's stricken machine, which slowed so dramatically that Nowlin overran it. As he pulled alongside the German fighter he realised that he needed to preserve fuel. Waving at Schack, Nowlin then climbed away. Schack subsequently bailed out, and the American Nowlin was not to learn of his kill for another 40 years. At the same time, two pilots gave chase to a Ju 88 that dived steeply away – so steeply that they were credited with shooting it down.

John Pugh's flight was uneventful until the very end. He was coming in to land at Piryatin, in the Ukraine, when he realised that he was going to overshoot the airfield. His Mustang was settling fast, so he pushed the throttle forwards and tried to go around, but his engine simply coughed. It was only then that Pugh remembered leaving his mixture in lean so as to conserve fuel, and this meant that the engine lacked the power to pull away. He shoved the mixture lever to 'rich' just in time to clear a group of women and their threshing machine. Years later, Pugh said he could

still remember the looks on the women's faces as he roared overhead at just 30 ft.

At Piryatin the group awaited its groundcrew, but none of them ever made it to the base from Poltava. As a result, many of the Mustangs were filled with low-grade fuel by Russian groundcrews, which made it hard for the machines to reach full power. One pilot crashed on take-off the next day but was only slightly injured. The fuel woes also meant that the group was strung out as it escorted bombers to Krakow. Even so, Capt John Pugh, Maj John Storch and Lt 'Bud' Nowlin reported achieving kills during the mission. In fact the Bf 109 that Storch shared with Nowlin saw the former achieve ace status.

On 8 August the group set out on the second leg of the shuttle, travelling to Foggia, in Italy, via Rumania. Bill Overstreet did not expect to see any action, so he traded his ammunition for vodka, which was stored in the empty bays. Inevitably, the group sighted Bf 109s over Rumania and the enemy fighters quickly broke for home. Overstreet got on the tail of one of the fleeing fighters and, to the American's amazement, the pilot bailed out. Overstreet was the nearest and could have been given credit for the fighter's destruction, but he was not.

Four days later the group provided an escort for bombers heading for southern France, although this time the Mustang pilots flew on to England.

Soon the regular missions were back on again, and the first of these that resulted in kills for the group came on 18 August. As pilots from

Lt Bill Overstreet's second *BERLIN EXPRESS* had been Capt 'Bud' Anderson's P-51B-15 43-24823 *OLD CROW*. When the latter pilot went on leave in July 1944 Overstreet was assigned his aircraft. One of the last P-51Bs in service with the 357th FG, 43-24823 was written off by Lt William S Davis in a landing accident on 30 May 1945 *(Olmsted via Roeder)*

P-51B-10 42-106462 *U'VE HAD IT!* was the mount of Capt John England, who had scored 7.5 victories by D-Day, when his aircraft received its invasion stripes. England would not score again until August, by which time he was flying a P-51D. On 4 October 42-106462 lost its tail assembly during a training flight, but its pilot, Lt Richard Potter, managed to bail out safely *(Olmsted via Roeder)*

the 357th FG made skip and dive-bombing attacks on a target north of Paris, elements of the 362nd FS found two Bf 109s and shot them both down. Capt John England claimed a share in one of them with a pilot from another group, this being the ace's first kill in almost three months.

Bad weather kept the 357th on the ground until 24 August, when it flew a bomber escort mission to Magdeburg. Near the target, Blue Flight of the 364th FS sighted a formation of six Bf 109s preparing for an attack on their charges. 'We chased them for several minutes and got into a firing position directly behind their formation', said Lt Harry Hermansen. 'Lt Gerald Tyler, flying Blue Three, picked the enemy aircraft on the right rear and I picked the enemy aircraft on the left rear'. Hermansen's Bf 109 disintegrated in mid-air and future ace Tyler sent his down in flames.

Following yet more miserable weather, the group's score rose once again on 13 September during a mission to Halle. The 364th was east of Frankenhausen when about 40 enemy aircraft burst out of the haze and plunged head-on through their formation. Only one German fighter was able to fire, albeit an inaccurate burst. After the initial gaggle went past, Maj John Storch spotted four Bf 109s about a mile behind the others and he turned Red Flight into them. He reported later;

'When we got within range they broke left and went into a turning circle. We turned three or four times with them and they began to break up. I followed one of them, firing, but I do not believe I got any strikes as he was taking evasive action and I was shooting poorly. He finally straightened out and went for an open field, and I got some strikes just before I overshot. He bellied in and caught fire when he hit.'

As Storch and wingman Lt Robert Schimanski re-formed, yet another Bf 109 came towards them. Storch broke into him and he 'turned with him a couple of times, firing while on the deck. As we got into a pretty nice position on the enemy aircraft's tail, I saw tracers all around us and then noticed we were above a camouflaged airfield. We broke off the enemy aircraft's tail and got up to about 3000 ft and circled around. The Me 109, meanwhile, circled on the deck within the perimeter of this airfield. Suddenly, he made a break for a larger field about a mile north of this airport. We dove on him and he started to belly in. As he hit we fired and he slid into a tree and exploded, throwing debris some 50 ft into the air.'

Storch and future six-kill ace Schimanski shared the credit for shooting down this fighter.

Capt John England was leading the 362nd FS when he spotted a single Bf 109 below him. He explained what happened next;

'I immediately dove toward him. The enemy pilot then saw me and started a break into me, and was headed for a large aerodrome. I was travelling at approximately 400 mph and made a very tight turn into him and closed to about 500 yards. I placed the enemy aircraft properly within my K-14 gunsight and squeezed the trigger. I got strikes all over the engine and

Maj Tommy Hayes and his crew pose with *Frenesi* in August 1944. The scoreboard displays Hayes' full tally of 8.5 victories scored with the 357th, plus two strafing kills achieved against the Japanese in 1942 (*Olmsted via Roeder*)

Four pilots from the 362nd FS assume a tight formation for the camera aircraft in the early autumn of 1944. The pilots and P-51D-5s are, from front to back, Capt Harvey Mace in *Sweet Helen II* (44-13558), Capt Calvert Williams in *WEE WILLY* (44-13334), Lt Thomas Martinek in *Pitter Pat* (44-13719) and Lt Charles Goss in *Screamin' Demon* (44-13596). 44-13719 was downed by flak over Koblenz on 30 December 1944, Lt Harold D Chandler being killed (*Olmsted via Roeder*)

cockpit. The enemy aircraft, burning and smoking, went out of control and crashed into a river from a height of 1000 ft.

'About 20 minutes after my first encounter, I was leading my squadron up to escort the last box of bombers. We were jumped by more than eight Me 109s at 15,000 ft. I tacked onto three of them that were spiralling toward the deck. I lined up on the leader's wingman and closed to about 300 yards and started firing. He tried both left and right evasive turns but his efforts were in vain. Finally, he made a tight pullout on the deck and cut his throttle. I cut my throttle and finished him off, closing to 100 yards. His canopy came off, smoke and pieces flew by and he rolled over and exploded in some woods below.

'I then made a 180-degree turn and caught another Jerry who was very aggressive. We spent five minutes in a tight Lufbery at tree-top altitude before I finally got into position for my first burst. I observed strikes around his tail section and one of his wheels dropped. I overshot him and pulled up sharply. My wingman, Lt Sam Fuller, came in and got some good strikes on him and the enemy aircraft started smoking. My wingman overshot and I came back and was getting strikes on him when he crashed into the side of a hill and exploded.'

New pilots, and future aces, Flt Off Otto Jenkins and Lt John Kirla of the 362nd FS each downed an enemy aircraft and shared in the destruction of a third. The 363rd FS was also in on the action, Lt Yeager sighting a Bf 109 near Kassel. He reported;

'I rolled over and I caught the enemy aircraft on the deck. I closed up fast and started firing at around 300 yards. I observed strikes on his engine and fuselage. The engine started smoking and windmilling. I overshot. Lt Frank Gailer fired at him until the enemy aircraft attempted to belly in, whereupon it exploded when it hit the ground.'

A total of 15 Bf 109s fell to the group's pilots, but five P-51s failed to return as a result of engine problems, flak or enemy fighters – the group would never lose more than five aircraft in a single day, although it reached this figure on three occasions. One of those lost was Lt Kirby Brown of the 364th FS, who succeeded in bailing out near Bad Frankenhausen after his Mustang was hit by flak, only to be captured and murdered by a *Sturmabteilung* officer.

From 17 September the group covered the airborne landings of Operation *Market Garden*. No trade was found on the offensive's first day, but on the second Maj Thomas Gates' force of 50 Mustangs experienced plenty of action. He reported;

'Over the drop zone we saw a gaggle of '109s and '190s flying to the right of us on a reciprocal course about 2000 ft above us. I turned the group right to intercept and called "Drop tanks" after clearing the gliders beneath us. By the time the tanks were off and we had started climbing, the first gaggle of '190s was passing overhead and up into the sun.'

When it was apparent that the Fw 190s would not bounce the group, Gates turned his Mustangs to attack. 'The fight was on', he said. Lt Gerald Tyler was leading the 364th's White Flight when he sighted a large gaggle of enemy aircraft in the distance. He reported;

'We turned to bounce them and when halfway there I saw the sun glistening off other bandits above them at approximately 20,000 ft. I turned away from the lower box and began climbing, but was bounced by about eight Fw 190s before I could reach their altitude. Picking the

Lt Frank Gailer chats with his crew on the wing of P-51C-1 42-103002 *JEESIL PEESIL MOMMY*, named after his flight school roommate's pet name for his wife. Gailer scored three shared victories while flying this machine but never made a full claim with the fighter (*USAF*)

Lt Col Irwin Dregne runs up P-51B-5 43-6510 *DAM-PHY-NO!*, which was not the machine assigned to him, at the start of another mission. The aircraft suffered engine failure and crashed into a field of Brussels sprouts shortly after taking off on the 18 September mission to Holland. Its pilot, Lt Norbert Fisher, suffered only minor injuries, but the Mustang was written off (*Roeder*)

centre Fw 190, I pulled the nose up and met him head-on. I fired a long burst, observing strikes all over his fuselage and centre section. He began burning and went straight down past me into the ground. Shortly afterwards, I saw a lone P-51 chasing an Me 109 and covered him until the P-51 shot him down. Then an Me 109 came in firing and slid past my nose. I followed him into a Lufbery, and after about four turns was able to draw deflection on him. I fired until he began burning and went into a spin. As I turned off him, another Me 109 came in on us and I broke into him. He used no evasive manoeuvres except violently skidding, and headed for the deck. I fired until the smoke was so thick I could no longer see him and then watched him crash in a small clump of woods.'

Tyler had bagged three German fighters in just a matter of minutes to 'make ace', these successes being added to his previous three kills. Future 364th FS ace Lt Robert Winks and his wingman, Lt Robert J Fandry, broke into several flights of Fw 190s and scattered them, but then Winks saw two more approaching them from behind. He waited to call the break then threw his aircraft into a steep turn, but Fandry failed to return. He had been killed when his P-51D crashed near the village of Svelen. Fandry had fallen victim to 112-victory ace Major Kurt Bühlingen, commander of JG 2.

The 357th was given credit for the destruction of 26 enemy aircraft during the melee, with Lt Arval Roberson accounting for two to take him to 'acedom'. Soon-to-be aces Maj Ed Hiro and Lts Charles Weaver and John Kirla each downed one, while Lts Frank Gailer and Harold Hand of the 363rd shared a kill.

Things got even hotter on 19 September, with the group fighting three distinct squadron-sized actions as pilots covered transports dropping supplies and men into the Arnhem area. The 364th FS was patrolling southeast of Arnhem when it tangled with enemy aircraft. Three Mustangs were lost but eight German fighters were destroyed. One of them represented the first kill for future ace Chester Maxwell.

Six-kill ace Lt Arval Roberson flew two *Passion WAGONs* in the ETO, and this was the second of those machines, P-51D-5 44-13691. It was the only one to display the large pin-up inspired by an image in *Esquire* magazine. Roberson 'made ace' in this aircraft on 19 September 1944 when he downed two Bf 109s over Holland. Once Roberson had completed his tour with the 364th FS in late September 1944, 44-13691 was passed on to future eight-kill ace Lt Charles Weaver (*Olmsted via Roeder*)

The 362nd's pilots heard frantic transmissions indicating a fight was in progress and they headed for it. They came across a battle between German and US fighters several miles away in an arena-like opening in the clouds. Arval Roberson took his four fighters to the edge of the engagement, and when he sighted a lone Bf 109 below him he banked over and fired. Flames began pouring from the cockpit and it fell away towards the ground.

Moments later Roberson and his wingman, Lt Charles Goss, saw another Bf 109 that had just made a firing pass on a P-51. The ace let off a short burst and saw bullets tear into the Bf 109's tail. He pulled more lead and let fly a burst that punched holes in the German aircraft's nose, releasing a stream of coolant and smoke. Roberson kept firing, but felt a stall coming on. He pushed his fighter to the left and levelled out, but when he turned back towards his target it was gone.

At Roberson's 'ten o'clock' was another Bf 109 in a steep climb. He called for Goss to take him but the latter did not respond, or move towards the German fighter. Roberson banked after it and tried to turn hard enough to get a shot at the enemy aircraft. Suddenly, strikes exploded all over the Bf 109 – another P-51 had cut across the turn and destroyed it. Roberson broke hard right to avoid the other Mustang. Later, Goss confirmed the destruction of the second Bf 109, which was Roberson's sixth kill. He too was now an ace.

The 363rd encountered 12 Bf 109s coming towards them from their 'three o'clock' position. Unknown to the Mustang pilots, these aircraft, from 7. and 8./JG 11, had sighted a single F-5 Lightning reconnaissance aircraft and were diving to intercept it. The hunters were about to become the hunted as the 363rd turned and dived to intercept them.

Maj Ed Hiro, flying the final scheduled mission of his tour, dived into a swirling Lufbery of 25 aircraft. A Bf 109 broke from the circle,

Capt Don Bochkay leads the 363rd FS escort in company with B-24J Liberator 44-40437 *HAIRLESS JOE* of the 493rd BG's 861st BS over England in the early autumn of 1944. Bochkay is flying his assigned aircraft, P-51D-5 44-13681. This machine was later transferred to Lt Michael Emery, who crashlanded it at Leiston on 31 December 1944 (*Olmsted via Roeder*)

Maj Ed Hiro was shot down and killed on 19 September 1944. Having 'made ace' just minutes earlier, this mission was scheduled to be the last of his tour (*Olmsted via Roeder*)

with Hiro on its tail. Flt Off Johnnie Carter followed, and he saw the Messerschmitt crash and burn. It was Hiro's fifth victory. The Mustangs turned back towards the Lufbery but Carter became separated from Hiro, who called on the radio to ask where the rest of his flight was. Leutnant Richard Franz of 7./JG 11 saw Hiro shoot up another Bf 109 as he closed on the Mustang ace, and he in turn hit the P-51D in the engine and cockpit. Lt Ted Conlin then went after Franz but it was too late. As the German pilot watched his

victim go down, Conlin stitched Franz's Bf 109G-14/AS across the engine and left wing, forcing him to crash-land in a wooded area. Hiro's Mustang slammed into the ground, killing its pilot.

The 362nd also ran across this largescale dogfight between III./JG 11 and the 363rd FS. Flt Off Otto Jenkins and Lt Walter Perry were approaching when two Bf 109s flew past their noses in neat formation. 'Lt Perry took the one on the right and I went after the one on the left', Jenkins said. 'I closed and began to fire. I saw many hits on the wing roots, canopy and wings. The aeroplane exploded and went into the ground. I saw no parachute'. Jenkins and Perry, now flying at low altitude, then sighted a single Fw 190 flying parallel to a railway track and they dived to intercept. Before Jenkins could fire, however, the Fw 190 pulled up, rolled, clipped a group of trees and crashed into the ground in a ball of fire. The squadron claimed a total of eight kills, with additional victories being credited to future aces Lts John Kirla and 'Chuck' Weaver.

In two days the 357th FG had downed 45 enemy aircraft at a cost of seven aircraft, with three pilots killed, two captured and two evading. It had been a rewarding, yet painful, set of missions.

CO of the 363rd FS since June 1944, Maj Ed Hiro flew a pair of Mustangs named *HORSE'S ITCH* during his time in the ETO. He was flying this machine, P-51D-5 44-13518, when he was killed in action on 19 September. Despite claiming 25 victories on this date, the 357th FG lost five Mustangs, with two pilots killed, two as PoWs and one evader (*Olmsted via Roeder*)

The sad end of *JEESIL PEESIL MOMMY* after Lt Frank Gailer ground-looped it at Leiston on 26 September 1944. Gailer's next mount was P-51D-4 44-11331 which he named *Expected* in honour of his pregnant wife (*Olmsted via Roeder*)

HUNTING THE LUFTWAFFE

Following 48 hours of hectic activity over Arnhem, the 357th FG saw no action for the next 17 days as losses were made good and replacement pilots were posted in to Leiston. Finally, on 6 October, the group was back over Berlin. As the Mustang pilots flew northwest of the German capital, Capt Richard Peterson's flight saw a large group of Luftwaffe fighters attack the box of bombers behind them. Lt Gilman Weber reported;

'We immediately dropped our tanks and turned to engage them. I spotted an Fw 190 and gave chase. He was quite a bit below me and I got too damned eager. I closed in on him as he levelled off at about 5000 ft. I realised I was over-running him and lowered flaps as I pulled alongside him. The '190 started a sharp turn to the left and evidently saw "Pete" Peterson coming in because he immediately jettisoned his canopy and bailed out.'

Peterson was given credit for the victory, taking his tally to 11.5 kills. The 362nd scored the bulk of the day's victories, with the successful pilots including Capt John England (two Bf 109s destroyed) and Flt Off Otto Jenkins (an Fw 190 destroyed).

Over Leipzig the next day the 363rd's pilots sighted enemy fighters 17,000 ft below them, and the squadron spiralled down to gain position. Lt Frank Gailer was trailing his leader, Capt Thomas Hughes, when an Fw 190 made a pass at the latter. 'I told Capt Hughes to hit the deck, and as the enemy aircraft passed in front of me I gave him one very short squirt', Gailer reported. 'As I turned to follow him he jettisoned his canopy and bailed out before I could fire again. I couldn't have fired more than 20 rounds on this one pass'.

Lt Arval Roberson's P-51D-5 *Passion WAGON* was passed on to future ace Lt 'Chuck' Weaver after the former was transferred home in late September 1944. And while Weaver had the name removed for some reason, groundcrew members were less enthusiastic about removing the nose art! By the time this photograph of 44-13691 was taken in late 1944 it had been transferred to the 364th FS (*Olmsted via Roeder*)

Don Graham led the 363rd FS from September to November 1943, then moved to group headquarters and took command of the 357th FG on 7 March after Col Henry Spicer was shot down and taken prisoner. Graham ultimately claimed one victory (on the day after he assumed command) and two damaged during his tour. P-51D-5 44-13388 *BODACIOUS* was his mount at the end of his tour, and following Graham's departure it was flown by Lt William J Currie as *Super X* and by Lt Peter Pielich as *Peter Beater*. The latter wrote the aircraft off in a crash-landing at Leiston on 3 April 1945 (*Olmsted via Roeder*)

Col Don Graham's tour as CO of the 357th FG ended on 10 October. It had been intended that group operations officer, and future ace, Lt Col Irwin Dregne would succeed him, but he was on leave at the time so ace Lt Col John L Landers, a veteran of the Pacific War and formerly CO of the 55th FG's 38th FS, stepped in as interim group CO.

On 12 October the 357th flew a mission to Bremen. The 363rd was briefed to act as the rover squadron, flying ahead and to the right of the first box of bombers. Over Steinhuder Lake, 22 Bf 109s crossed directly in front of the squadron. 'I was coming out of the sun and they were about 1.5 miles away at the same level', reported 'Chuck' Yeager, now promoted to lieutenant. However, before he could open fire two of the German pilots simply rolled over and bailed out. Yeager, who was given credit for the destruction of these aircraft, reported;

'I was the closest to the tail-end of the enemy formation and no one but myself was in shooting range. I dropped my tanks and then closed up to the last Jerry and opened fire from 600 yards. I observed strikes all over the ship, particularly in the cockpit. He skidded off to the left and was smoking and streaming coolant when he went into a slow diving turn to the left. I closed to within 100 yards of the next Me 109, skidded to the right and took a deflection shot of about ten degrees. I gave about a three-second burst and the whole fuselage split open and blew up after we passed. Another Me 109 to the right had cut his throttle and he was trying to get behind me. I broke to the right and quickly rolled to the left onto his tail. I got a lead from around 300 yards and gave him a short burst. There were hits on the wings and tail section. He snapped to the right three times and bailed out.'

Lt Yeager had just claimed five Bf 109s in as many minutes, making him the first pilot in the 357th to become an 'ace in a day'.

Two of Yeager's squadronmates also enjoyed success. 'My element leader, Lt Richard Roper, was shooting at two Me 109s when I told him to break left into a Me 109 that was coming in from "seven o'clock high"', explained Lt Frank Gailer. 'Being about 300 yards behind, I tried to pull up under the enemy aircraft – I pulled up sharply, fired one burst and snapped onto my back as I went above the German fighter. I saw him do a wingover and head down from 18,000 ft'. Gailer was credited with a single kill while Roper scored two to take his final tally to four victories.

The group's next chance to tangle with the Luftwaffe came on 2 November during an escort mission to Merseburg. When the bombers started their runs the 362nd turned to avoid the flak directed at them, planning to pick the 'heavies' up as they cleared the target area. 'As we were doing this, a single Me 109 came 180 degrees to us in a dive for the clouds', said 'Kit' Carson. 'Leading the last flight in our squadron at 15,000 ft, I immediately attacked to prevent his escape into the overcast. I began firing from 100 yards dead astern, closing fast. I fired continuously until closing to 30 yards, still dead astern. I got strikes on his cockpit and wing roots. The aeroplane rolled several times, going straight down out of control. I pulled off and watched him crash'.

Capt Richard Peterson, meanwhile, had his three-aircraft section circle until all the bombers had dropped their loads. He then made a sweep south of the target in response to a report of jet fighters in that area. Finding none, the flight returned, 'in time to intercept about 20 enemy aircraft making a pass at the last box', Peterson said. He went on;

'I couldn't get in an effective pass because there were so many fighters from the 352nd FG around. I finally hit the deck and came across a lone Fw 190 under the overcast. He saw me and started to climb. He turned to the left and I fired two bursts. I caught him with the second burst, hitting him from the nose to the cockpit. He spun away firing his guns and exploded when he hit the ground.'

Lt 'Chuck' Yeager was one of only two pilots in the 357th FG to 'make ace in a day', a feat he achieved on 12 October 1944 when he downed five Bf 109s (*Olmsted via Roeder*)

The only known photograph of Capt 'Kit' Carson's short-lived P-51D-15 44-14896 *NOOKY BOOKY III*. The ace received this machine after he had passed P-51D-5 44-13316 *NOOKY BOOKY II* on to Lt 'Ted' Conlin. The latter renamed the aircraft *Olivia de H* after actress Olivia de Havilland (*Olmsted via Roeder*)

A windblown Capt 'Kit' Carson poses with his groundcrew after the closest call of his combat career. A single bullet went through the side of *NOOKY BOOKY II* and hit the canopy release, sending the canopy flying off into space and subjecting the ace to a cold and windy flight back to Leiston (*Olmsted via Roeder*)

The waist gunner of a 34th BG Flying Fortress took this photograph of Capt Richard Peterson's third *Hurry Home Honey* (P-51D-15 44-14868) after he and his wingman had formed up on the damaged bomber during late 1944 (*Olmsted via Roeder*)

Capt Peterson's second *Hurry Home Honey* (P-51D-5 44-13586) is seen here in the 364th FS's dispersal area at Leiston in the 'two-tone' Olive Drab over natural metal scheme unique to the 357th FG. Peterson had claimed 13.5 of his 15.5 victories by the time this photograph was taken in mid-October 1944 (*Olmsted via Roeder*)

On 6 November, during an escort mission to Minden, the group encountered a new enemy aircraft type. North of Osnabrück, White Flight of the 363rd spotted a trio of Me 262 jet fighters flying in the opposite direction to the Mustangs on their right-hand side. And another flight called in two more below, flying the same course as the American fighters. Capt Yeager was White Flight leader, and he reported;

'I turned my flight to the right and headed the last man off. I fired off a 90-degree deflection burst at an Me 262 from 400 yards. I only got a hit or two on him before he pulled away. We were flying above an overcast that was very thin. I went down under it and flew along for a minute or two until I met them head-on again, only they were now flying at about 2000 ft. I split-ess'ed on the leader and they all separated, and I fired a high-deflection burst from above at the leader. I got behind him and fired two or three bursts and got hits on the fuselage and wings from 300 yards. Then he pulled away and went into the haze and I lost him.'

Yeager, now separated from his flight, soon saw an airfield, and before long 'I spotted a lone Me 262 approaching the field from the south at 500 ft. He was going very slowly at around 200 mph. I split-ess'ed and fired a short burst from around 400 yards and got hits on the wings. I had to break off at 300 yards because the flak was getting too close. I broke straight up and, looking back, I saw the jet crashland about 400 yards short of the runway in a wooded field'.

The 363rd went hunting for targets on the airfield at Villingen on 18 November. Capt Robert Foy was leading White Flight when he spied eight German aircraft orbiting the field. The ace later reported;

'I dove to intercept and pulled up on the tail of a Me 109 who was on approach with its wheels down. I lowered flaps and gave the enemy aircraft a short burst. Hits were observed on the fuselage and the enemy aircraft dove into the trees on the northeast edge of the airfield. I pulled up to the right and manoeuvred onto the tail of another Me 109, also with wheels down. I again lowered my flaps and gave him another short burst of fire, observing strikes on the left wing (*text continues on page 64*).

COLOUR PLATES

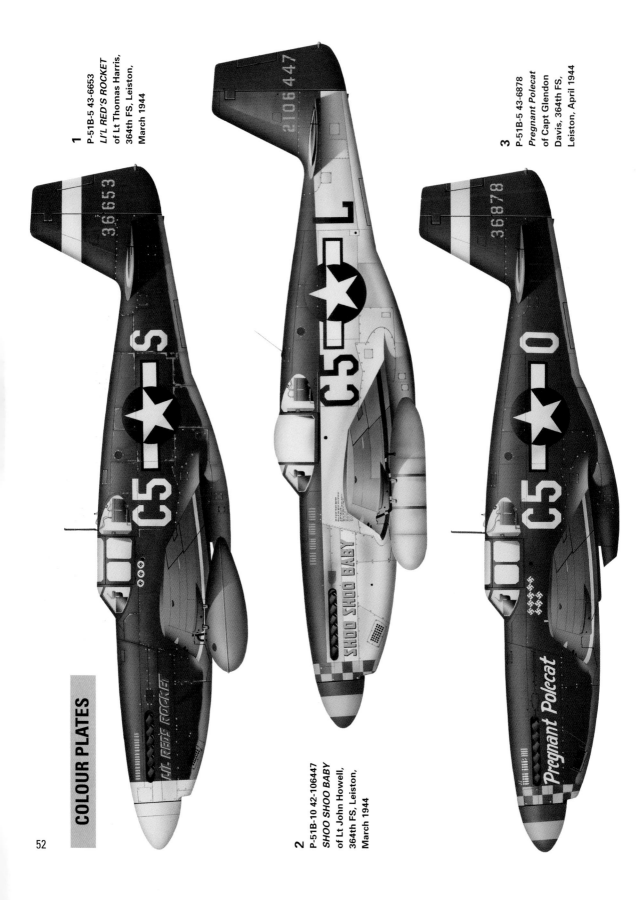

1
P-51B-5 43-6653
LI'L RED'S ROCKET
of Lt Thomas Harris,
364th FS, Leiston,
March 1944

2
P-51B-10 42-106447
SHOO SHOO BABY
of Lt John Howell,
364th FS, Leiston,
March 1944

3
P-51B-5 43-6878
Pregnant Polecat
of Capt Glendon
Davis, 364th FS,
Leiston, April 1944

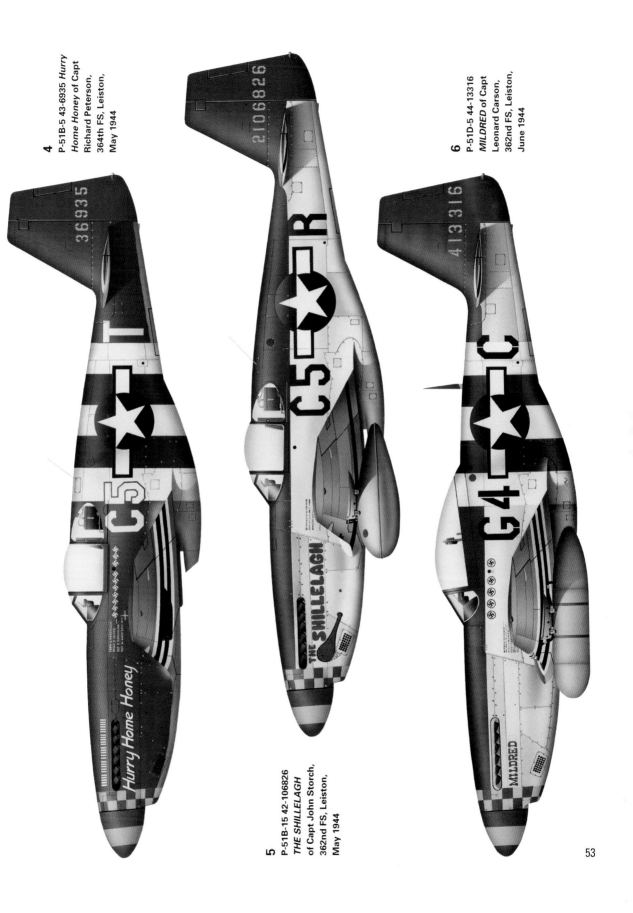

4
P-51B-5 43-6935 *Hurry Home Honey* of Capt Richard Peterson, 364th FS, Leiston, May 1944

5
P-51B-15 42-106826 *THE SHILLELAGH* of Capt John Storch, 362nd FS, Leiston, May 1944

6
P-51D-5 44-13316 *MILDRED* of Capt Leonard Carson, 362nd FS, Leiston, June 1944

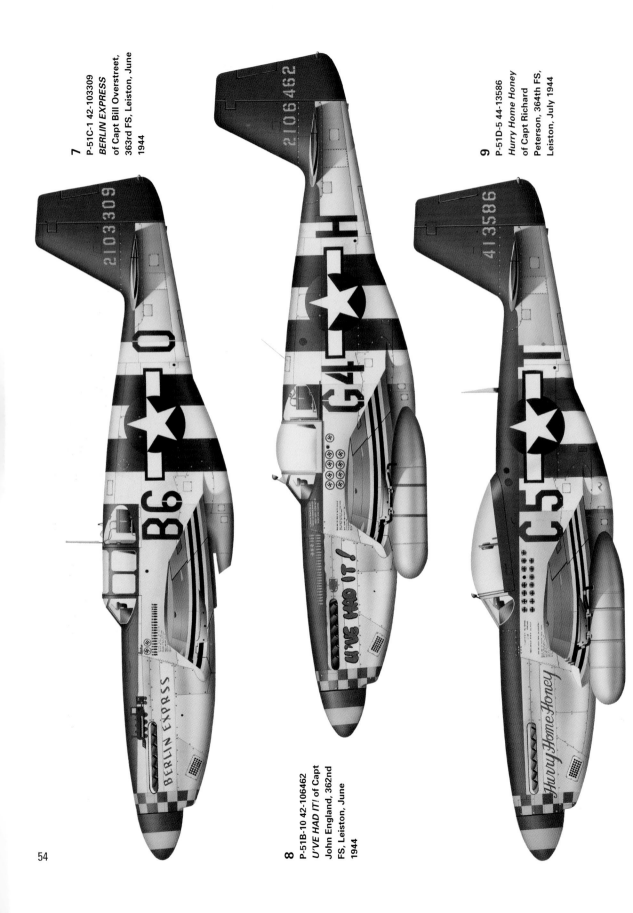

7
P-51C-1 42-103309
BERLIN EXPRESS
of Capt Bill Overstreet,
363rd FS, Leiston, June
1944

8
P-51B-10 42-106462
U'VE HAD IT! of Capt
John England, 362nd
FS, Leiston, June
1944

9
P-51D-5 44-13586
Hurry Home Honey
of Capt Richard
Peterson, 364th FS,
Leiston, July 1944

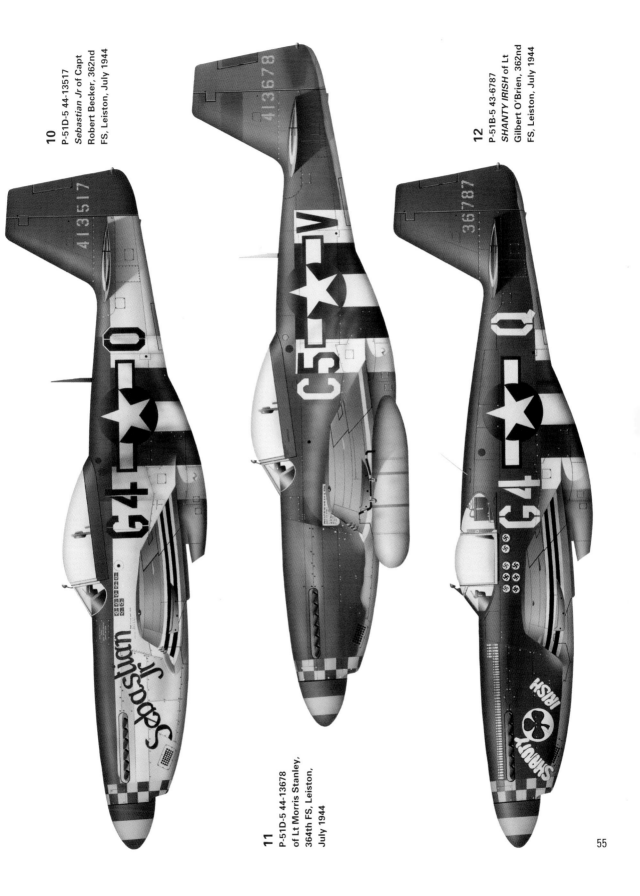

10
P-51D-5 44-13517
Sebastian Jr of Capt
Robert Becker, 362nd
FS, Leiston, July 1944

11
P-51D-5 44-13678
of Lt Morris Stanley,
364th FS, Leiston,
July 1944

12
P-51B-5 43-6787
SHANTY IRISH of Lt
Gilbert O'Brien, 362nd
FS, Leiston, July 1944

55

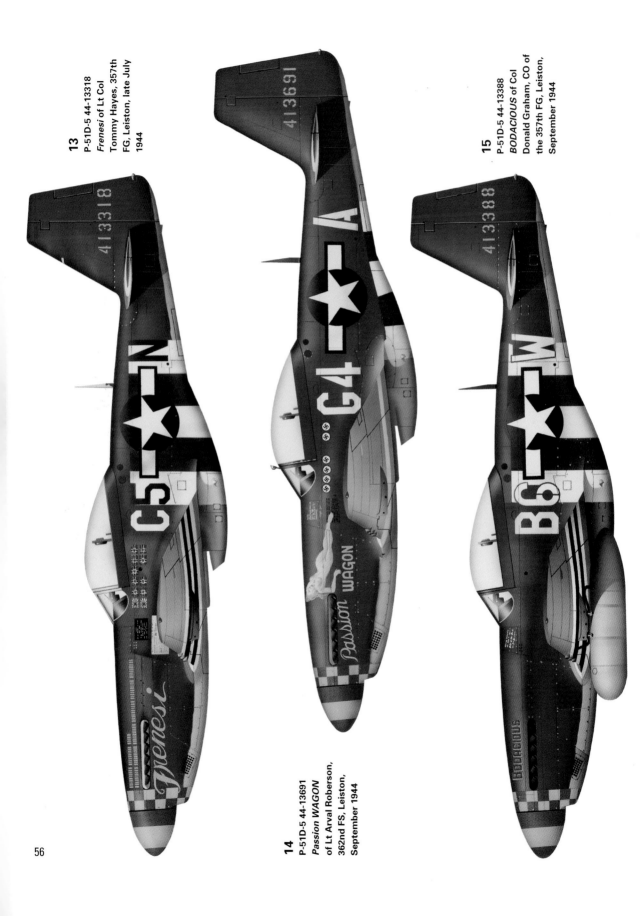

13
P-51D-5 44-13318
Frenesi of Lt Col
Tommy Hayes, 357th
FG, Leiston, late July
1944

14
P-51D-5 44-13691
Passion WAGON
of Lt Arval Roberson,
362nd FS, Leiston,
September 1944

15
P-51D-5 44-13388
BODACIOUS of Col
Donald Graham, CO of
the 357th FG, Leiston,
September 1944

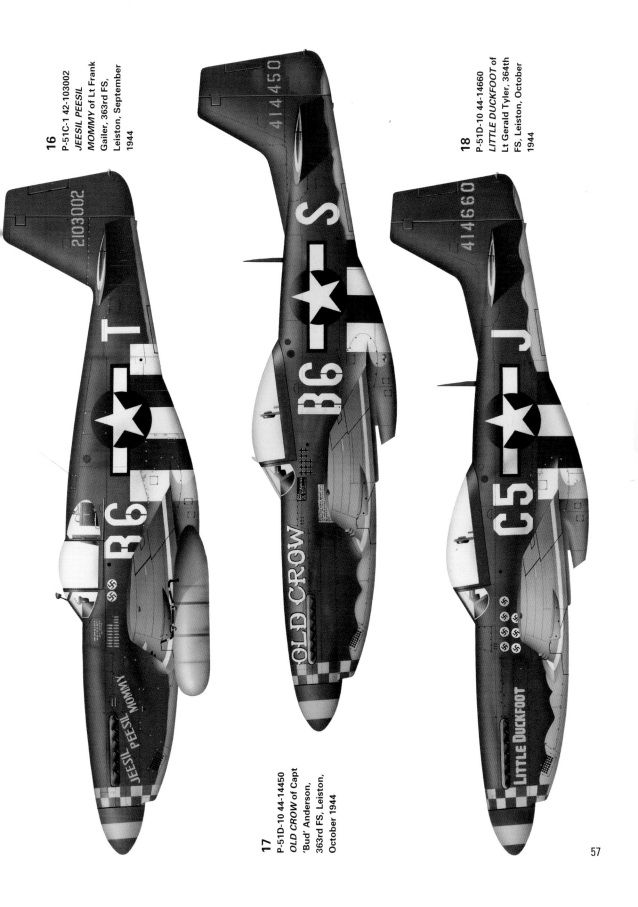

16
P-51C-1 42-103002
JEESIL PEESIL MOMMY of Lt Frank Gailer, 363rd FS, Leiston, September 1944

17
P-51D-10 44-14450
OLD CROW of Capt 'Bud' Anderson, 363rd FS, Leiston, October 1944

18
P-51D-10 44-14660
LITTLE DUCKFOOT of Lt Gerald Tyler, 364th FS, Leiston, October 1944

57

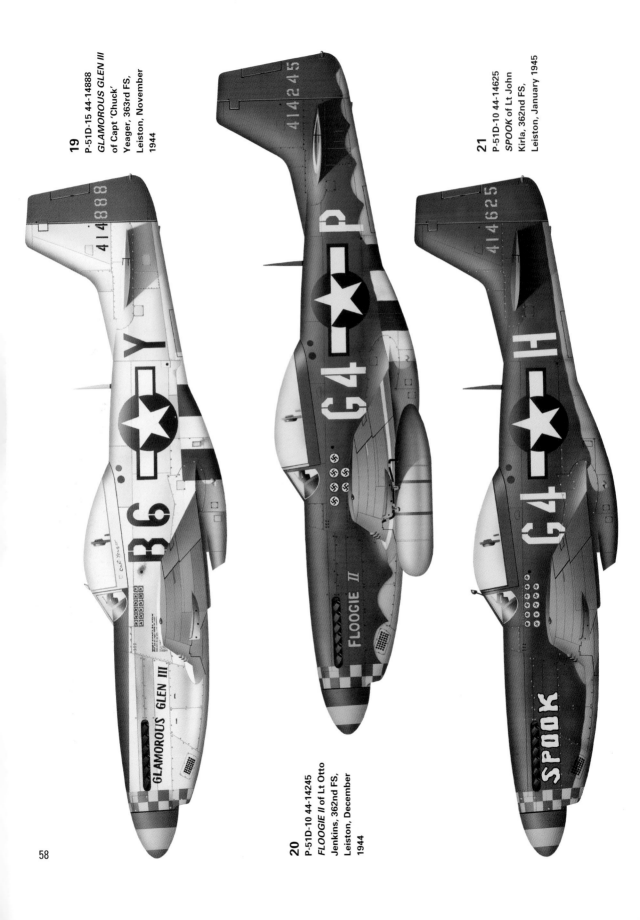

19
P-51D-15 44-14888
GLAMOROUS GLEN III
of Capt 'Chuck'
Yeager, 363rd FS,
Leiston, November
1944

20
P-51D-10 44-14245
FLOOGIE II of Lt Otto
Jenkins, 362nd FS,
Leiston, December
1944

21
P-51D-10 44-14625
SPOOK of Lt John
Kirla, 362nd FS,
Leiston, January 1945

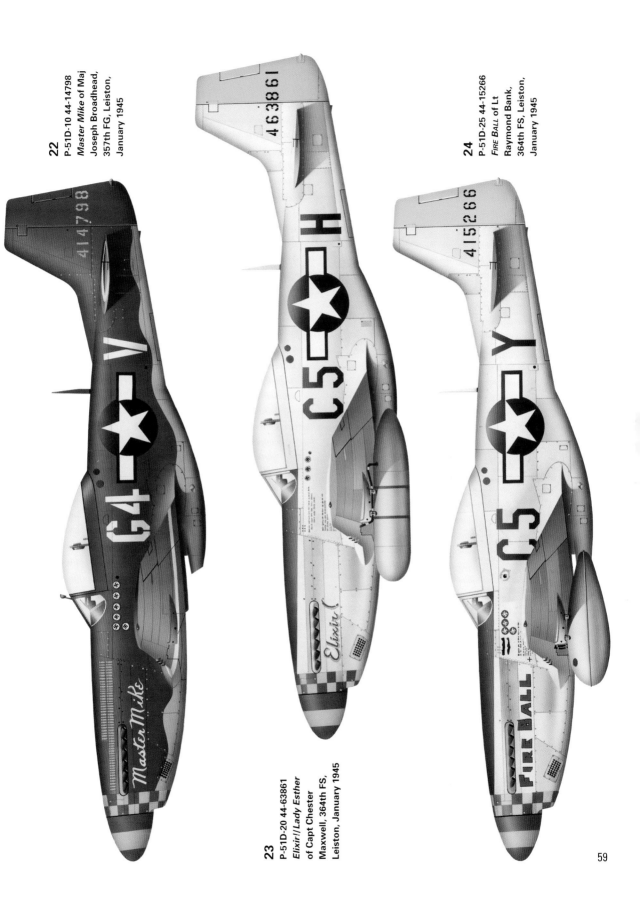

22
P-51D-10 44-14798
Master Mike of Maj
Joseph Broadhead,
357th FG, Leiston,
January 1945

23
P-51D-20 44-63861
Elixir·I/Lady Esther
of Capt Chester
Maxwell, 364th FS,
Leiston, January 1945

24
P-51D-25 44-15266
Fire Ball of Lt
Raymond Bank,
364th FS, Leiston,
January 1945

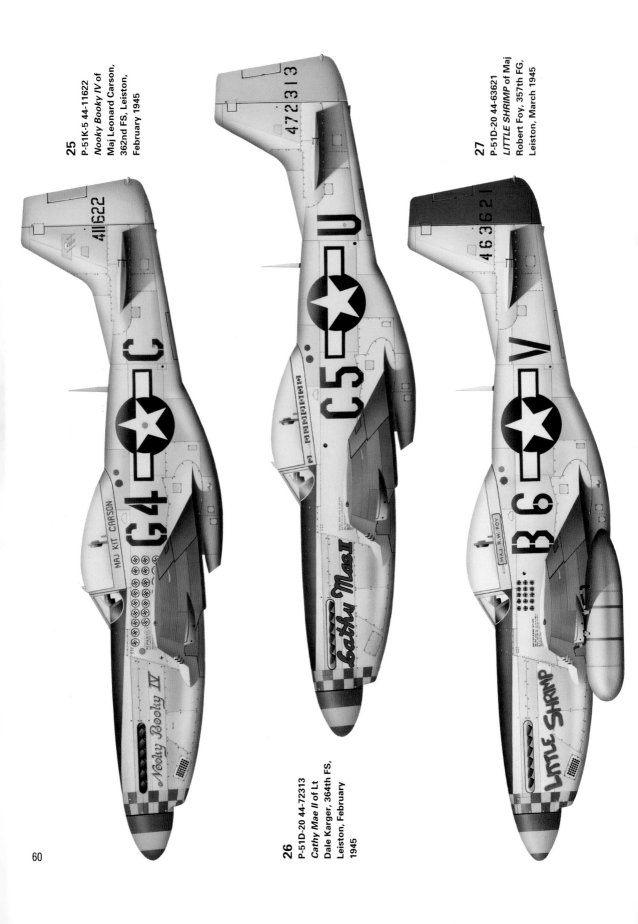

25
P-51K-5 44-11622
Nooky Booky IV of
Maj Leonard Carson,
362nd FS, Leiston,
February 1945

26
P-51D-20 44-72313
Cathy Mae II of Lt
Dale Karger, 364th FS,
Leiston, February
1945

27
P-51D-20 44-63621
LITTLE SHRIMP of Maj
Robert Foy, 357th FG,
Leiston, March 1945

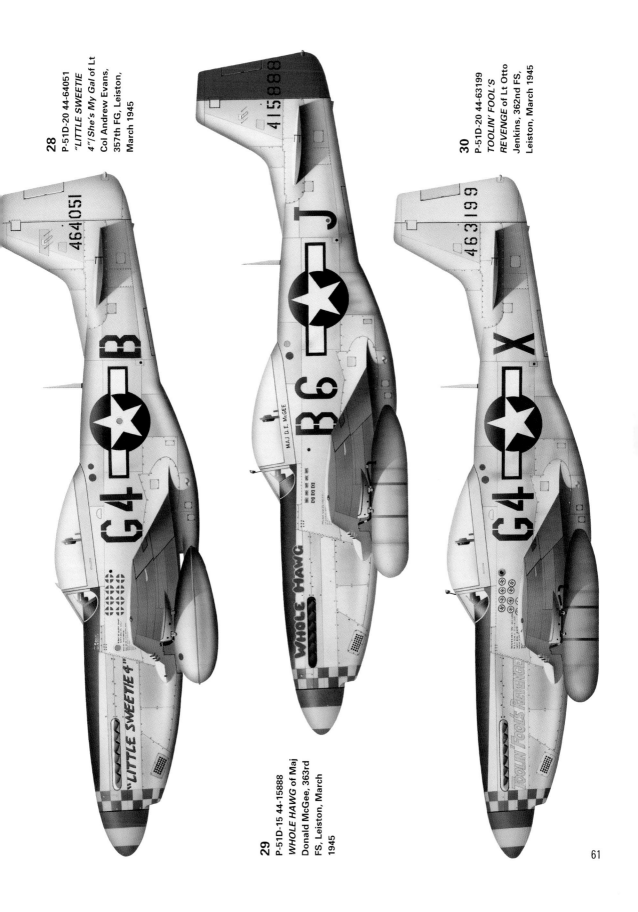

28
P-51D-20 44-64051
"LITTLE SWEETIE 4"/She's My Gal of Lt Col Andrew Evans, 357th FG, Leiston, March 1945

29
P-51D-15 44-15888
WHOLE HAWG of Maj Donald McGee, 363rd FS, Leiston, March 1945

30
P-51D-20 44-63199
TOOLIN' FOOL'S REVENGE of Lt Otto Jenkins, 362nd FS, Leiston, March 1945

61

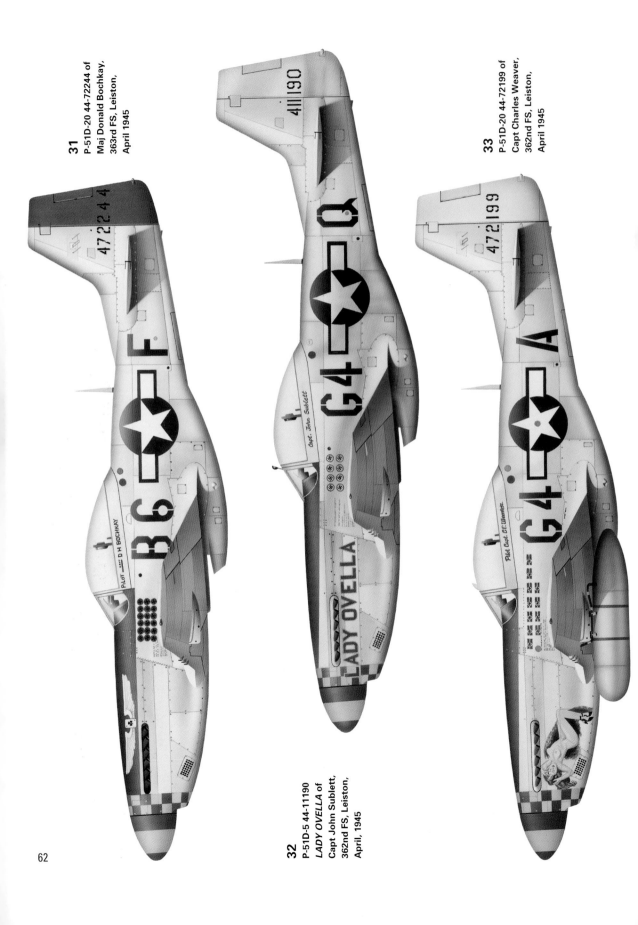

31
P-51D-20 44-72244 of
Maj Donald Bochkay,
363rd FS, Leiston,
April 1945

33
P-51D-20 44-72199 of
Capt Charles Weaver,
362nd FS, Leiston,
April 1945

32
P-51D-5 44-11190
LADY OVELLA of
Capt John Sublett,
362nd FS, Leiston,
April, 1945

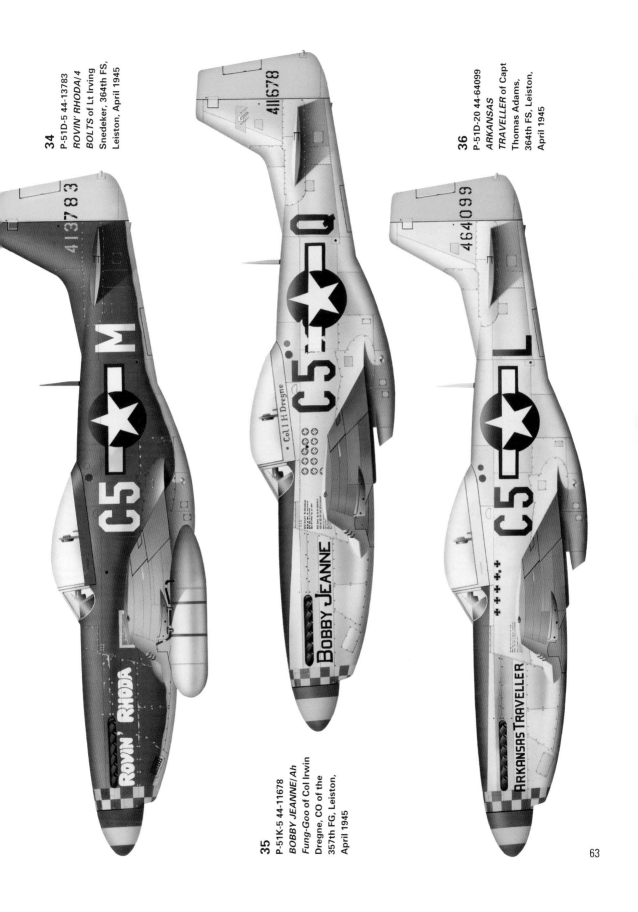

34
P-51D-5 44-13783
*ROVIN' RHODA/4
BOLTS* of Lt Irving
Snedeker, 364th FS,
Leiston, April 1945

35
P-51K-5 44-11678
*BOBBY JEANNE/Ah
Fung-Goo* of Col Irwin
Dregne, CO of the
357th FG, Leiston,
April 1945

36
P-51D-20 44-64099
*ARKANSAS
TRAVELLER* of Capt
Thomas Adams,
364th FS, Leiston,
April 1945

He immediately pulled his wheels up and started a turn to the left. I followed him through several 360-degree turns, getting hits with several different short bursts. Smoke started streaming out of the left side of the Me 109 and he made a sharp turn to the right. Just as he made the sharp turn, Lt Henry Hare, my No 2 man, turned sharply inside of me and fired a burst, hitting the enemy aircraft on the right wing.'

Lt Robert Winks' flight was hunting for enemy road traffic when he spotted a Bf 109 on the deck approaching his flight head-on. 'I dropped down on his tail from 5000 ft and proceeded to chase him over hill and dale'. Winks fired a burst from close range that shattered the canopy and hit the engine and cockpit. The German pilot – probably Unteroffizier Karl Weitzel of 5/JG 53 – bailed out, suffering a broken leg in the process. This was the first of Winks' 5.5 victories. Lt Col John Landers also scored. He had claimed six victories in P-40Es while defending Australia and fighting in New Guinea in 1942, plus four more while flying with the 55th FG in 1944. Landers' Bf 109 on this date was his sole victory with the 357th, and he would go on to claim 3.5 kills leading the 78th FG. He also finished the war with 20 strafing victories to his name, including one during this mission – indeed, a number of 357th FG aces claimed strafing kills at Villingen, Mengen and Neuhausen airfields on 18 November.

Finally, Capt Richard Peterson also downed a Bf 109G-14, probably flown by Obergefrieter Heinz Gruber of 5/JG 53, during the mission. Although wounded, Gruber survived.

On 27 November the group, and especially Capt 'Kit' Carson, had a big day at the Luftwaffe's expense. Two large formations of German fighters were reported near Magdeburg, records showing that these machines came from JG 300 and JG 301. 'One of the formations made a turn and came toward us from "eight o'clock"', Carson said. 'We dropped our tanks and turned to meet them. We tacked onto the rear of the formation, which consisted of 50+ Fw 190s. I closed to within 300 yards of the nearest one and fired a medium burst with no lead, getting numerous strikes. He started to burn and went into a turning dive to the left. I believe the pilot was killed. He never recovered, crashing into the ground and exploding'.

Carson returned to the main formation, again closing on the last aircraft;

'I opened fire at about 300 yards, firing two short bursts and getting strikes all over the fuselage. The fighter started to smoke and burn. He dropped out of the formation and turned to the right until he was in sort of a half split-s position, never recovering from this attitude. I saw him crash and burn. The pilot did not get out. Closing again on the main formation, I pulled into the nearest man. At about 400 yards

Lt Col John L Landers was something of an itinerant group commander during 1944-45, but he called the 357th his own in October and November 1944. As was the case during his time with other groups, he christened the Mustang (P-51D-5 44-13923) that he flew with the 357th *Big Beautiful Doll*. Landers scored single aerial and strafing victories with the group on 18 November 1944 (*Olmsted via Roeder*)

I fired a short burst, noting a few hits. He broke violently to the left and I broke with him. I picked up a lead on him and fired two more bursts, getting strikes on the cockpit and engine. He started to smoke and burn badly. The pilot jettisoned his canopy and bailed out. The Focke-Wulf crashed about 50 yards from a house in a small town.

'I could still see the main formation about a mile ahead of me. Starting to catch them, I saw a straggler on the deck. I dropped down to engage him but he saw me coming. He turned left away from me and I gave chase for about three minutes before I caught him. I opened fire at about 400 yards, getting strikes on the right side of his fuselage. He turned sharply to the right and I picked up a few degrees of lead, firing two more bursts and getting more strikes on the fuselage. The pilot jettisoned his canopy and bailed out.

'I pulled up and had set course for home when another Fw 190 came in at my wingman and me from "seven o'clock high". We broke into him and started a zooming climb. I chased him, gaining slowly. Suddenly, he dropped his nose and headed for the deck. I gave chase and caught him in four or five minutes. I opened fire at 400-450 yards but missed. I closed further and fired another burst, getting several strikes on the fuselage. The aeroplane started to smoke. I fired again as he made a slight turn to the right, observing more hits on the fuselage. Then the pilot jettisoned his canopy and I broke off my attack to the right. I waited for him to bail out but he didn't, so I turned back to engage him again. I was still about 700 yards away when the pilot pulled the nose up sharply and left his ship. His 'chute opened a couple of seconds later.'

Capt Carson had just become the second, and last, 357th FG pilot to make 'ace in a day'. His tally now stood at 11.5 kills.

Future ace Maj Andy Evans of the group's HQ flight saw an Fw 190 turning in an attempt to flee. 'I turned as tight as I could, rolled to the left and down, firing as I came out of the turn. Before I could fix my sights on him and get off a good burst, he rolled into the ground from 1500 ft, exploding as he hit'.

Former instructor, recent Leiston arrival and future eight-kill ace Lt John Sublett was flying on Capt John England's wing when they spotted 40 to 50 Fw 190s just below them at about 'ten o'clock'. 'I pulled up behind the rearmost enemy aircraft and closed to within 600 yards, at which point I opened fire and saw strikes around his cockpit, with smoke and fire coming out around his engine nacelle', recalled England. 'The enemy aircraft flipped over and the pilot bailed out'. Continuing to close on the gaggle, England picked out a second Fw 190 and fired again from just 300 yards. 'He broke, but I got good hits on his wings and cockpit while he was breaking, and during one or two turns immediately after this break his canopy and pieces of his wings came off. The pilot bailed out, but I believe he was seriously injured'.

Even triple aces were not immune to flak. Capt Leonard 'Kit' Carson examines the damage to *NOOKY BOOKY III* after a strafing attack on Mengen airfield on 18 November 1944. Carson claimed a Bf 109 destroyed (one of 3.5 strafing victories that he would ultimately be credited with), but his aircraft – near-new P-51D-15 44-14896 – was so badly damaged by flak in return that it had to be written off (*Olmsted via Roeder*)

Assigned to the 357th FG's HQ flight, Maj Andy Evans claimed the first of his six kills on 27 November 1944. The group's only West Point graduate, he had joined the 357th the previous month following a combat tour in Iceland (*Olmsted via Roeder*)

Sublett saw England cull the first two Fw 190s from the formation and 'was busy covering his tail, expecting the Jerries to break into us, but they just kept going and stayed in formation', he said. England continued his attack on the gaggle as it dived for safety, picking off another Fw 190. Sublett reported;

'He flipped over and went straight into the ground. The pilot was definitely killed. Then I pulled up behind another Fw 190 and went through the same procedure, starting to fire from 800 yards and closing to 150 yards, observing strikes on his cockpit. The aeroplane dove straight forward, went into the ground and exploded. Capt England finally called me and said that he only had three guns left. He then instructed me to shoot at the remaining Fw 190s. I pulled up on the tail of one of the fighters and fired a short burst from about 800 yards but missed. Another Fw 190 cut across between us and I tacked onto him because he was closer. I fired from about a ten-degree angle from 400 yards, observing strikes all over the ship. Pieces started coming off and the pilot jettisoned his canopy, pulled up and went over the side.

'I pulled over to dead astern behind another Fw 190 and fired from about 600 yards, closing to about 500 yards, observing strikes at the wing roots and fuselage. Many pieces started flying off and the canopy went under my right wing. The pilot pulled up and sailed over the side. I broke to the right, just in case anyone was on my tail, and fell in behind another Fw 190. I pulled up to approximately 500 yards and fired a long burst that went under him. I raised my sights and fired another long burst. The enemy aeroplane just disintegrated. I had to pull up to avoid the flying debris.'

'This was one of the best shows I have ever seen', England gushed. The squadron's aces had indeed had a field day, as aside from Carson's five, England claimed four, Sublett three and Capt Alva Murphy and Lt 'Chuck' Weaver two each.

Lt Robert Schimanski had been leading the 364th south of Brandenburg when flak diverted the group, and this meant that the squadron arrived too late to enjoy the same levels of success as the 362nd FS. Nevertheless, Schimanski lost no time in diving 'into five enemy aircraft circling around at 15,000 ft, losing my own flight. I pulled in sharply behind an Me 109, spanned him and gave him a short burst, hitting him at the wing root.

Capt John England's last and perhaps best-known Mustang was P-51D-10 44-14789 *MISSOURI ARMADA*, named after his home state. England wrote on the back of this photograph, 'This aeroplane completed more than 30 missions over Germany without an abort. The man chiefly responsible for this aeroplane's consistent record was SSgt Robert Currie. He was a wonderful crew chief and a credit to our great unheralded groundcrews'. The fighter later became Lt Oscar Ridley's *Sad Sack*, and he was shot down in it by flak whilst attacking airfields near Prague on 18 April. Ridley successfully evaded (*USAF*)

Capt 'Chuck' Yeager's final Mustang in the ETO, P-51D-15 44-14888 *GLAMOROUS GLEN III*, displays his full scoreboard of 11.5 victories. Upon Yeager's repatriation in January 1945, 44-14888 became *Melody's Answer*, and it was lost to flak over Haseloff on 2 March. Its pilot, Flt Off Patrick L Mallione, perished (*Olmsted via Roeder*)

On the second burst I cut the left wing off and the enemy aircraft snapped over on its back as I overshot'.

At around this time Capt Yeager heard another group call 'bandits' and the 363rd FS duly turned left and spotted two 'gangs of enemy aircraft, one consisting of 50+ fighters and the other of approximately 150+. I passed in front of the little gang and climbed over the back end of the large bunch to 32,000 ft. I jumped the last enemy aircraft, which was an Fw 190. He went into a rolling dive to the right. I fired a deflection shot from his right and got hits from around 200 yards. He snapped and the tail flew off. I saw no 'chute.

'I then pulled back up into the bottom of the gang and was jumped by another Fw 190. I broke into him and got a deflection shot from 90 degrees at around 100 yards. I got many strikes on the fuselage and the enemy aircraft started smoking and went into a dive. I followed it down to about 15,000 ft and the enemy aircraft flew apart. I climbed back up to the tail end of the gang and jumped another gaggle. The enemy aircraft started a circling turn with me and I turned inside and closed up to within 100 yards at around 40 degrees of deflection. I fired a short burst concentrated on the cockpit – a sheet of flame came out of the cockpit and the aircraft nosed down in a dive on fire. There was no 'chute.'

In the same melee, Lt Frank Gailer of the 363rd FS was lost. He had just downed two Fw 190s to 'make ace' when two more aircraft made a head-on pass at him. He thought they were Mustangs, but they opened fire, knocking off his canopy, cutting his oil lines and wounding him in the shoulder. 'I heard Lt Gailer say that he was shot up and oil was coming over his windshield', reported Yeager. Gailer was last seen about 15 miles southwest of Magdeburg. He was captured and spent the rest of the war as a PoW.

'Bud' Anderson also scored two victories, taking his tally to 14.25 kills. In one of its most productive days in terms of aerial victories, the

357th FG had claimed no fewer than 31 German fighters destroyed on 27 November.

On 2 December the group covered bombers striking Koblenz. 'We were approaching Bingen when 15-20 Me 109s initiated an attack from "five o'clock", recalled 'Kit' Carson. 'We dropped our tanks and turned into them. I singled out a flight of three. They dropped beneath the haze and I closed on tail-end Charlie, firing a burst at 350 yards and getting strikes on the fuselage. I closed a bit further and fired another burst, getting more strikes. Pieces came off his ship and it started to smoke. He went into a tight spiral to the right and crashed. The pilot did not get out. I turned to attack the remaining two '109s. They split and I followed what I thought was the leader as he dived for the deck. I closed in to about 400 yards and fired a burst, getting no hits. I closed further and fired a long burst, getting strikes all along the left wing and fuselage. He started to smoke and burn. He was about 20 ft above the river. He pulled up and headed for a field on the other side. He made the field but did a half roll at about 100 ft and went into the ground. Again, the pilot did not get out.'

Capt Alva Murphy heard Carson's call to drop tanks. He later reported;

'My flight leader went into the clouds, where I promptly lost him. When I came out of the clouds I was sitting on the tail of two Me 109s at about 1000 yards. I opened fire on one of them and got strikes. He started smoking as I closed to about 600 yards, and I fired another long burst, observing many strikes. Pieces began falling off of the enemy aircraft. Then the Me 109 went into a spin and exploded upon hitting the ground. Lt Herman Delager, who was flying behind me, shot down the second Me 109, whose pilot remained in perfect formation while I was shooting his partner down.

'I started climbing from the deck to gain altitude. At about 8000 ft, I spotted another lone Me 109 about 1000 yards distant and headed 180 degrees from me. I broke towards him, intending to give chase, but evidently he saw me as I made my turn and was afraid to fight. The pilot promptly rolled his ship over and bailed out.'

Mugging for press cameras at Leiston in late 1944 are the 357th FG's leading aces – Capt Richard 'Pete' Peterson, Capt Leonard 'Kit' Carson, Maj John England and Capt Clarence 'Bud' Anderson. Between them they shot down 67.75 German aircraft and, almost as remarkably, all four aces survived the war (*USAF*)

Two more aircraft were also downed that day, one of which was a lone Ju 88 ambushed by Capt Robert Foy for his ninth victory.

Three days later, during a mission to Berlin, 'Bud' Anderson's flight flew in advance of the bomber stream to break up any attacks forming ahead of it. 'We intercepted about 20 Fw 190s', he reported. 'They broke around and I picked one out, firing a burst and getting good hits all over. He rolled over and I did not follow as there were too many enemy aircraft around'. Anderson's wingman, Lt James Sloan, said, 'I do not believe the enemy aircraft ever recovered from this spin as the pilot was either killed or the controls shot away'. Soon, Anderson spotted four more Fw 190s darting in and out of the haze. He later recalled;

'I fired and they all broke left and I latched on to the No 4 man, firing a long burst at close range. The canopy blew off and fire belched from the cockpit as it spun straight down into a broken overcast. I then closed on the No 3 man, fired at good range and more good hits occurred in the cockpit region. This ship spun down smoking, out of control.'

Lt James Browning spotted two Bf 109s ahead of him. 'I was coming practically head-on when they saw me and dropped their belly tanks. I made a turn to the left to get on their tails and they broke into us. I took the second, and with the K-14 gunsight made quite a deflection shot. I observed hits on the engine and cockpit. He went into a spin and the pilot bailed out'.

As the bombers reached the target another gaggle of fighters rose to challenge them. The 362nd was in position to intercept, as Carson explained;

'Two ships at the very front of their formation were the first to break. I broke with them and fired on the leader, getting several strikes on his fuselage. He made a dive for the clouds. I chased him but inside the clouds I couldn't see him. I broke out into the open, and a few seconds later tracers were breaking around my ship. I broke to the right as hard as I could. The Jerry was right behind me, but quite a distance back. I managed to get into a scissoring turn, making several head-on passes. He finally reversed his turn and I tagged onto him, firing another burst at about 200 yards. Closing fast, I saw more strikes on the fuselage. Then, in a tight spiral, the Me 109 went down through the overcast. I went beneath the overcast and saw the burning wreckage.'

Maj Joseph Broadhead was leading the group. He spotted ten to fifteen enemy aircraft below a thin layer of cirrus and led the jump, hitting an Fw 190 from very close range. Broadhead lost sight of his victim, but his wingman, Lt Myron Becraft, saw the Fw 190 go straight into the ground and explode. Lt John Kirla picked out one enemy aircraft, opening fire at about 700 yards and 'getting strikes at his wing roots and on his fuselage. The aeroplane began streaming smoke and pieces flew off as I closed to 50 yards, getting more strikes. I believe the pilot was killed, for the Me 109 went straight down in a dive at terrific speed and hit the ground and exploded.

'After I had destroyed the Me 109, Lt Sublett and I stooged around the deck, looking for more enemy aeroplanes. We spotted a lone Fw 190 on the deck and gave chase, catching him in two to three minutes. I got on his tail and fired a long burst from 700 yards, getting strikes on the fuselage and tail. Suddenly, the pilot rolled his ship over and bailed out.'

Lt Otto Jenkins of the 362nd FS enjoyed great success during the final months of 1944, claiming 8.5 kills between 13 September and 24 December. He was killed when his fighter hit trees on 24 March 1945 during a low-level beat up of Leiston at the end of what was supposed to be his final operational mission (*Olmsted via Roeder*)

It was at this point that Lt Matthew Martin noticed fluid coming from Kirla's Mustang. He moved in for a closer inspection and was sprayed with fuel – the P-51D had a leaking tank. As he radioed Kirla to tell him to switch tanks, the fuel spraying Martin's aircraft ignited. He dived to try to extinguish the blaze but to no avail. He then climbed to bail-out altitude. When Martin tried to escape from the cockpit, the aircraft snap-rolled and trapped him half in and half out. Pushing with both hands, Martin managed to propel himself from the cockpit but his thigh hit the horizontal stabiliser. His parachute opened, and upon landing Martin did his best to avoid being taken prisoner by the Germans. However, with an injured thigh restricting his mobility, he was easily captured.

Despite excessive fuel loss, Kirla's aircraft remained airworthy and he made it home. The 357th had claimed 22 victories for the loss of two aircraft. Aside from the aces already mentioned, Capt Don Bochkay and Lt Dale Karger each claimed two kills, while Lts Thomas Adams, Paul Hatala and Robert Schimanski were credited with one apiece.

On 23 December the group flew two missions – escorting bombers and a photo-reconnaissance Spitfire – which netted Capt Robert Foy two kills and Lt 'Chuck' Weaver and Flt Off Saul Sitzer a victory apiece.

Christmas Eve brought no respite as the group was briefed to escort bombers to Babenhausen. A large formation of Fw 190s was spotted near Fulda and the two aircraft flying as spares with the 362nd broke into them. One Mustang was lost in the process – one of three P-51s lost during this clash, all of which cost the lives of the pilots involved.

Red Flight saw the German formation pass below them on a reciprocal course. 'I did a wing-over and dove into the rear of the gaggle', said Lt Otto Jenkins. 'I picked out an Fw 190 and at 300 yards began firing from dead astern. I got numerous strikes and he exploded at the cockpit. The pilot did not get out. I selected another Fw 190, who started evasive action. I closed to 200 yards, firing numerous bursts and getting many strikes all over his fuselage. He turned to the left and the pilot bailed out. Singling out another Fw 190, I commenced firing from

Lt Col Irwin Dregne (right) was an original member of the group, but he briefly served with the 363rd FG as its Operations Officer between March and May 1943. Returning to the 357th FG, he would eventually become its final wartime CO (*USAF*)

A crewman poses on the wing of Col Irwin Dregne's P-51D-5 44-13408 *BOBBY JEANNE/Ah Fung-Goo II* at Leiston (*Olmsted via Roeder*)

500 yards, closing in to 100 yards and getting strikes on the wing roots and cockpit. When I overshot to the right, the pilot rolled over and bailed out.

'There were still plenty of enemy aircraft around, so I latched onto my fourth Fw 190. While I was trying to get a shot off, however, a '190 slid onto my tail and began firing.'

Jenkins' aileron and compass were damaged. He added;

'My wingman, Lt Edward Hyman, shot him off. The aeroplane snapped over and went down, and I saw either the canopy or the wing fall off it. Then I managed to get a shot at the Fw 190 in front of me. I saw hits on the wing and cockpit. He started smoking and went into an uncontrollable spin and crashed.'

These four victories made Otto Jenkins an ace.

Meanwhile, in the battle fought by the 362nd's pilots, Lt John Kirla added three more to also attain ace status, and 'Kit' Carson and Lt Col Dregne got one each. The 363rd knocked down six fighters, although none fell to aces, and the 364th was also involved when Lt Robert Winks led his flight down on the enemy. 'I caught an also-diving Fw 190, gave him two bursts and he bailed out', recalled Winks. But he had not yet emptied his fuselage tank so the imbalanced Mustang snapped out of control and the stick went slack in Winks' hands. The diving Mustang went into the compressibility region, forcing the young pilot to chop his throttle and then slowly recover the aircraft when it entered the thicker air near ground level. Winks added in his combat report that 'my praying' had also been involved. Other future 364th aces to score kills included Lts Raymond Bank, Dale Karger and Robert Schimanski. In all, the group had again downed 31 enemy aircraft. By comparison, the rest of 1944 was uneventful.

Lt Tom Adams shared in the destruction of an Fw 190 with Lt Irving Snedeker on 5 January to score the group's first victory of 1945 during a patrol in the Kassel area, and five days later he shot down a Bf 109 over Paderborn airfield.

The group's first big action of the year would come on the 14th, when it claimed a record tally that resulted in the creation of four new aces.

'BIG DAY' AND AFTER

On 14 January 1945 the 357th FG was briefed to provide cover for bombers attacking the German town of Derben. The mission would come to be known in group lore as simply 'Big Day'. Lt Col Irwin Dregne was leading, escorting the first three boxes of bombers, when he spotted two large groups of contrails ahead;

'I led the 364th FS towards the contrails, instructing the other two squadrons to stay close to the bombers. As I got closer to the contrails, I noticed a large gaggle coming in at our level, and they turned out to be Fw 190s flying company front formation in waves of eight. The contrails I first spotted were Me 109s providing top cover.'

Amazingly, the top cover turned away from the Fw 190s, leaving them completely exposed. Dregne ordered the 364th to drop tanks.

'The '190s broke formation and scattered, some of them rolling, some split-ess'ing, but the majority broke right and then went into a Lufbery. I got my sights on a '190 and started firing, observing strikes on the fuselage and tail. He broke left and then went into a spin. I broke left, finding myself in a Lufbery with eight or ten Fw 190s. I started a tight climbing spiral, the '190s following, but I was able to out-climb them. I noticed a bomber box under attack so I started climbing toward it. When I got to the box the fight was over and the Huns had left. I picked up a P-51 and told him to be my wingman.'

Lt Col Andy Evans was flying the Mustang, and he had already shot down a Bf 109. He flew another Fw 190 into the ground and then climbed after a third Fw 190, which abruptly collided with a fifth German aircraft to make him an ace. 'I then spotted an Me 109 below me at 20,000 ft', Dregne continued. 'I chopped my throttle, slid in behind it and started firing. I observed strikes around the cockpit, and the

Col Irwin Dregne poses in the cockpit of the first *BOBBY JEANNE/Ah Fung-Goo,* P-51K-5 44-11678. His crew chief chose the name on the right-hand side of the nose, while that on the other side was in honour of Dregne's wife and daughter. The colonel was flying this aircraft on Christmas Eve 1944 when he destroyed a Bf 109 near Koblenz to achieve his fourth kill. He would claim another Bf 109 with it on 14 January 1945 to 'make ace' (*Olmsted via Roeder*)

Lt Otto 'Dittie' Jenkins' P-51D-10 Mustang 44-14245 *FLOOGIE II* displayed the name on both sides of the nose. It was belly-landed in December, repaired and crashed near Leiston on 13 January, killing Lt Robert Schlieker (*Olmsted via Roeder*)

aeroplane started smoking and burning, spinning down. The Me 109 crashed'. Dregne too was now also an ace.

Maj John Storch singled out an Fw 190 and his opponent broke for the deck. 'I followed him from 24,000 ft straight down to 2000 ft', he explained. 'He was taking wild evasive action. I did not think I was hitting him, but at 12,000 ft smoke began to pour out of the enemy aircraft. As I broke off, my wingman observed black smoke coming from the Fw 190 and saw him hit the ground'. As Storch recovered from his dive, he spotted a fight below him;

'I singled out an Fw 190 on the outside of the scrap and he went for the deck. I followed, and at this point my wingman observed an Fw 190 firing at us and he had to break off to take care of him. In the meantime, my Fw 190 was going balls-out on the deck. I had enough excess speed to pull up behind him and fired for some time with no effect. I finally managed to get close enough so I couldn't miss and saw the strikes centre on the fuselage and left wing. He burst into flames and suddenly snap-rolled, and large pieces flew off. I overshot, and he went into the ground burning. I did not observe the pilot get out. I pulled up and my wingman pulled off his '190, and we rejoined.'

Before they could regain altitude they sighted two Bf 109s below them and dived to attack yet again. Storch said;

Maj John Storch admires the nose art on his third *THE SHILLELAGH* (P-51D-20 44-72164) which was assigned to him after his second mount (P-51D-5 44-13546) was shot down on 5 December 1944 with Capt Herman Zetterquist at the controls. 364th FS CO, Storch achieved four victories while flying 44-72164, including two on 'Big Day' (*Olmsted via Roeder*)

'They separated and hit the deck. I picked one and chased him for about five minutes. I finally caught him and he went into a turning circle. My gunsight had burned out and I was a picture of confusion trying to turn, fire, fix my sight, put down flaps, pull up flaps and work my throttle. Finally, I once again got close enough so I couldn't miss and got strikes – coolant and smoke came from the enemy aircraft. He tried to belly in just short of a forest, hit and bounced almost over into a clearing but then struck the last few trees on the fringe of the forest.'

Meanwhile, White Flight of the 364th FS dived into the same mass of aircraft. Capt Tom Adams was amongst those to enjoy success in the swirling dogfight that ensued;

'There were so many fighters it was hard to pick a single target, but I caught one coming head-on and gave him a burst as he came by. I swung around and he gave me a good demonstration of snap rolls, then went into a rolling dive for the deck. My airspeed was past 450 mph when the '190 snapped and disintegrated. He went into the ground and exploded. No 'chute was seen. As I pulled away I lost my wingmen, and I was trying to pick them up when I noticed an aeroplane circling around all alone. No one else was in the area, so I started after him.

'Situating myself between him and the sun, I poured on the coals and chased him for about 15 minutes. I thought I was never going to catch the bastard. Apparently he thought he was safe because he throttled back. I closed and had to put down full flaps in order not to overrun him. My first burst hit him in the port wing root and he sort of turned as if to look behind him, but I was still between him and the sun and he levelled out again. This time I turned on the heat, getting hits in the cockpit and blowing his canopy off. He turned on his back and went straight in from 10,000 ft.'

These were Tom Adams' final victories, and he ended his tour with 4.5 aerial kills and one strafing victory.

Blue Flight's Lt Paul Hatala climbed with two Fw 190s whose pilots were foolish enough to head for the bombers. He picked out one and fired, sending it spinning away in flames, then went into a turning fight with the other one. 'He split-ess'ed and went down to the deck. I followed him, and after he did a couple of manoeuvres I got into position and gave him another burst of fire. Trailing flames, I saw him crash into the ground'.

Yellow Flight was down to two fighters because of aborts. Yellow Leader, Lt Robert Winks, lost his wingman in the initial turn towards the fighters. 'I found myself making a head-on pass at an Fw 190, guessed the lead, fired and observed many strikes on the engine, cockpit and left wing root', Winks explained. 'I wheeled around just in time to see the left wing collapse up over the canopy. I didn't see the pilot get out'.

Winks circled to gain altitude and soon encountered another Fw 190 trying to make a head-on pass. 'He was damned aggressive so we started our affair with another head-on pass. Neither of us fired. Soon we found ourselves ess-ing back and forth on a common course, chopping throttle, adding throttle and dropping flaps, both trying to get the advantage. A sad situation! Finally, I out-ess'ed him, got on his tail, fired and he obligingly blew up'. Winks then climbed away and tried to find the rest of his flight.

'I heard my wingman say he was with the bombers over the target, so I headed off to join my squadron. I saw a lone Me 109 several thousand feet below me, with another lone Fw 190 several thousand feet below him. I thought it was a trap, so I cautiously began to drop down on the Me 109. He saw me coming and broke into me, whereupon I fired in another head-on pass and observed many strikes between the cockpit and tail. He lost control and started spinning. The '190 had made a turn and was now directly overhead. Soon I decided that the Fw didn't intend on coming down so I lit out for the '109 who had since regained control.

He started a turn to the left and, as soon as my range was correct, I gave him a rather long burst, observing a few strikes on the left wing. As soon as I had let up on the trigger his tail disintegrated.'

Winks was credited with 2.5 victories during the mission, taking his score to 4.5 – tantalisingly close to ace status. Meanwhile, an Me 262 made an ineffective pass at the 364th's Green Flight and accelerated away without taking any further action. Moments later Green Leader Capt Chester Maxwell sighted 25 to 35 Fw 190s. He was so eager to break up this group's attack that he simply peeled off and dived into the enemy formation without radioing the rest of his flight. Maxwell described what happened next;

'As I approached the formation, some of them broke to the left and the remainder split-ess'ed toward the ground. None reached the bombers. I got a 20-degree deflection shot in on one of the Jerries who broke to the left. I noticed several strikes around the centre of the fuselage and wing root. He started down, out of control and smoking. Almost immediately one wing came off and he burst into flames.'

Lt Raymond Bank, meanwhile, had attacked a formation of Fw 190s performing a defensive Lufbery turn manoeuvre. His first kill came when a Focke-Wulf overshot him, the future ace recalling;

'I closed to about 100 ft and set him on fire. I then jumped another Fw 190 and shot him down in flames. No pilot was seen to come out of the aeroplane. While looking for my flight, I bounced a '190 that gave me a hard time as I only got a few strikes on him in snap shots. He dove down and came up into a loop. At the top of it, he kicked it into a hammerhead so as to try to make a head-on pass. He was going fairly slowly at the top of it, and as he kicked over he gave me a perfect target. I continued firing until he burst into flames.'

Lt Dale Karger had also begun to turn with the Lufbery. A few minutes later a Bf 109 dived for safety. 'I followed it' said Karger. 'I kept getting strikes on him over the tree-tops for about two minutes. He then belly-landed in a field and caught fire'.

Maxwell had been unable to reform the flight because of 'excessive chatter on the R/T', so he continued fighting alone. He reported later;

'I spotted 12 more '190s making a pass on the rear element of bombers from about "five o'clock". I bounced them and the entire group made

One of four men to 'make ace' on what became known as 'Big Day', Capt Chester Maxwell downed five enemy fighters in two missions. Aside from the three Fw 190s that he shot down on 14 January 1945, Maxwell had destroyed a Bf 109 and another Fw 190 over Holland on 19 September during the Operation *Market Garden* battle (*Olmsted via Roeder*)

a diving turn to the left, failing to penetrate the bombers. I climbed on another Jerry's tail, gave him one long burst and he flopped out of control, hit the ground and burst into flames. There was a fight going on down below me. I dove and attacked another '190 on the tail of a black-nosed P-51. I fired on him from 60 degrees in a head-on pass, closing to about 100 yards. I observed good strikes and the pilot bailed out.

'I then spotted a single '190 attacking the bombers. He split-ess'ed and I followed him down, gradually closing. At about 12,000 ft I looked back and saw another P-51 trailing me. Confident that I had my tail covered, I pressed the attack. The next thing I knew, I felt strikes on the aeroplane and my canopy was shot off. I tried my radio and evidently it was shot up as it was not working. My coolant gauge needle went up to 150 degrees and the engine began to smoke, and I figured he had also shot out my coolant. The P-51 then closed and I saw it to be a yellow-nosed job. He made no further passes at me but flew off. I cut my engine and put the aeroplane in a shallow glide. The canopy was off and belts of ammunition were hanging out of the wing. I made it back to Antwerp and bellied the fighter into an English Army parking lot.'

Despite the ignominious end to this sortie, Maxwell had tallied three Fw 190s destroyed, taking his overall score to exactly five victories. He too was now an ace.

Green Flight of the 362nd FS also engaged Fw 190s and Bf 109s as they attacked USAAF bombers northwest of Berlin, with ace Lt John Kirla exacting a particularly heavy toll on the enemy. 'I picked out an Fw 190 that was shooting at a formation of bombers and closed in to about 100 yards before I opened fire. I clobbered him all over. I believe I killed the pilot. I watched him dive inverted into the ground and explode. My second Fw 190 was in a dogfight. I closed on him and started to fire from about 400 yards down to about 50 yards, getting strikes all over him. He began to tumble and I watched him go into the ground.

'I looked around for another target and saw an Me 109 shooting down a bomber. I went after him, getting on his tail and closing to about 30 yards. He went into a very tight barrel roll going straight down. I fired a short burst and he straightened out. Then I really gave him the works. He flipped over on his back and started to burn. Pieces fell off the ship until, finally, just the framework remained. There wasn't enough of this ship left to crash into the ground.

'Looking around again, I observed two Me 109s flying 180 degrees to the bombers and a P-51 chasing them. The P-51 closed in and got the first Jerry, but the second one slid onto the Mustang's tail and shot it down. I was at close enough range by this time to get some revenge. I began firing at about 200 yards and played with him awhile. I soon got tired of that and opened up at about 50 yards. I filled him full of holes. Pieces started to fly off him and he went down like a falling leaf.'

Lt John Sublett was leading Yellow Flight when he spotted 'a long line of Me 109s in a sort of extended column containing six to ten aircraft abreast. They totalled at least 100. I told my wingman that when they finally got through passing by we would tack onto their rear end and start shooting. Finally, they passed by, and the last four Me 109s then broke into us. We started a honey of a Lufbery that lasted for about six turns. I finally cut the butter and got a short burst into one of them. I was going straight down when I fired from about 100 yards, seeing many strikes right into the pilot through the top of his canopy. The aeroplane went out of control and crashed into the ground'.

Another Bf 109 tried to dive away and Sublett shot it down to add to his score, thus 'making ace' in the process. By then the 362nd's White Flight had become a six-aircraft element because Majs John England and Joseph Broadhead had joined after their wingmen aborted. Now they spotted a formation of German fighters. England reported;

'The enemy aircraft made several orbits as though they were sizing up the situation. While they were debating, I placed my squadron in the proper position, hoping to break up the gaggle before they could attack the bombers. They did attack before I could get to them, but we interfered slightly and engaged the Krauts in individual dogfights.'

One Bf 109 slipped through and headed for the bombers. England got onto his tail, but he was out of firing range. He reported;

'The pilot displayed a little judgment by looking around. Then he put his ship in a 90-degree vertical dive from 32,000 ft. I followed him down. At about every 5000 ft during the descent, he would roll and do

Maj Joe Broadhead takes off in his P-51D-10 44-14798 *Master Mike* (right) in January 1945. Broadhead had claimed his fifth kill on 30 April 1944 and commanded the squadron until 25 August, when his first tour ended. He returned to Leiston in October as group operations officer, and it was at this point that he was assigned 44-14798. After Broadhead was repatriated for a second time in February 1945, the fighter was passed to Lt Julian H Bertram, who renamed it *Butch Baby*. Immediately post-war 44-14798 was stripped of its Olive Drab paint and renamed *Dainty Dotty* by pilot Lt James C McLane (*Olmsted via Roeder*)

some very violent evasive manoeuvres. I just did a tight spiral around him. At 8000 ft he made a tight pull-out and levelled off. Evidently he thought he had lost me, for he began flying straight and level. I started firing at 200 yards, closing to 50 yards. I got strikes all over the left side of the fuselage and left wing. Just before I released the trigger about four feet of the left wing ripped off. The pilot did not get out before his ship hit the ground and violently exploded.'

Broadhead covered England all the way down but an Fw 190 jumped onto his tail. The German pilot was so intent on shooting Broadhead down that he flew right in front of Lt Donald Cheever. After the latter had despatched Broadhead's pursuer, White Flight re-formed and Broadhead spotted a lone Bf 109, which he quickly destroyed. 'Pieces started coming off the enemy ship, then the canopy came off and the pilot bailed out', Broadhead said. 'I almost rammed the pilot'.

'Kit' Carson's Blue Flight was busy too. As soon as they spotted the fighters preparing to hit the bombers head-on, according to Carson he 'fired at them coming head-on, then turned and tacked onto the rear of the gaggle. Their attack on the bombers had been diverted, so I closed to about 400 yards on an Fw 190 at the rear on the outside and fired a good burst that hit home all over his fuselage. He took no evasive action, but just peeled down to the right very slowly. I followed him down. His turns became more violent and then he started snapping from the right to the left. He was smoking quite badly. I believe the pilot was killed. I pulled off and watched him until he hit the dirt.'

Another pilot in Carson's flight, Lt John Duncan, dived after two fighters and shot both of them down. While Duncan descended, Carson and the two remaining members of his element had climbed. 'I went back up to the bombers, looked straight back at "six o'clock" and saw 40 to 50 Fw 190s coming up about 1000 yards behind', Carson said. 'There were a couple of P-51s near me and they broke with me. We met the enemy head-on. They didn't fire but we did, although I saw no hits.

'After we got behind them, I fired a burst from 350-400 yards at an Fw 190, getting strikes. He did a couple of snaps to the right and wound up on his back. I fired again, getting more hits on the fuselage. Pieces came off the enemy ship and he began smoking. He split-ess'ed and headed for the deck. I followed him down until he hit, bounced and crashed.

'I had climbed back up to about 14,000 ft when two Me 109s came tooling by about 2000 ft beneath me. I dropped down and fired at the one in the rear, getting no hits. They dropped flaps and broke violently. I zoomed back up while they circled in a Lufbery. I made another ill-timed pass and pulled up again. The leader broke off and headed for the deck. I dropped down to tail-end Charlie as he started down. He pulled up, losing speed. I firing at about 300 yards, closing down to about 20 yards, and scored hits all over the fuselage. His coolant blew as I pulled up over him. Then he went into a sort of tumbling spiral and crashed.'

A Bf 109 dived between Lt Charles Weaver and his element leader, splitting them up. While he scrambled to rejoin he spotted another Messerschmitt. He quickly latched onto the Bf 109's tail and fired a short burst from long range. The enemy fighter responded with a steep left turn. Weaver was almost inverted when he fired. He saw no strikes, but

Totting up the final numbers on 14 January 1945, Lt Col Irwin Dregne (right) calculates the provisional score following the group's efforts on 'Big Day'. At left, aces Capt Robert Foy, Maj John Storch and Lt Col Andy Evans admire the tally. These four pilots alone had shot down ten fighters between them during the mission (*Olmsted via Roeder*)

the Bf 109 just dived straight into the ground. Claiming an Fw 190 a few minutes later, Weaver had also achieved 'acedom' during this epic clash.

The 363rd's pilots had seen the action begin. 'I saw aeroplanes exploding and spinning down in front of us', said Capt James Browning. He raced to join in and engaged the enemy. When the Messerschmitts dived on the bombers, ex-363rd FS pilot Capt Foy, who was now attached to the HQ flight, led his charges in to cut them off. He reported;

'The '190s broke their company front formation and headed in every direction imaginable. I turned to the right and lined up an Fw 190, giving him short bursts while in a shallow turn. After a few strikes he immediately straightened out for a second or two and suddenly the pilot jettisoned his canopy and bailed out. I pulled up sharply to avoid colliding with the Hun pilot, and as I flew over him I observed another Fw 190 flying 90 degrees to my path of flight and directly beneath me. I did a quick wingover and split-ess'ed onto his tail. The pilot apparently saw me closing in and did a split-s toward the deck. I followed him, giving him short bursts and observing strikes on the left wing. He continued his dive – I was following closely behind, and was indicating better than 550 mph. He made no move to pull out of his dive, so I started a gradual pull-out at about 4000 ft, but kept his ship in view off to one side. The enemy aircraft dived straight into the ground.'

Browning, meanwhile, 'saw a gaggle of 25+ Me 109s about 5000 ft below us and to the right. I led my flight down on them, positioning it at the rear of the enemy formation. I picked out an Me 109 on the right side and fired a burst, observing a concentration of hits on the cockpit and engine. The enemy aircraft did a violent snap roll and then spun down completely out of control. Meanwhile, an Me 109 had gotten on my tail, but my wingman, Lt James Taylor, shot him down. I picked out another Me 109 in front of me and fired three or four bursts from short range, observing many hits in the centre of the fuselage. Again, the enemy aircraft went into a violent spin, completely out of control. I then tacked onto another Me 109, which I followed as he broke right. I fired a short burst and observed hits. Before pulling up over him I fired a long burst as he was crossing in front of me, raking the enemy aircraft the length of the fuselage to the engine with a good concentration of hits. The enemy aircraft rolled over and went down out of control.'

In all, the group had posted the remarkable score of 56.5 victories for the loss of just three fighters (all three pilots survived as PoWs). It was the biggest single day tally for any US fighter group in the European Theatre of Operations, and four pilots – Maxwell, Sublett, Weaver and Evans – 'made ace'. Evans was one of only two West Point graduates to achieve ace status, the other being Col Morton Magoffin of the 362nd FG.

Two pilots who missed the show were 'Chuck' Yeager and 'Bud' Anderson, for this was to be the last mission of their tours and they were briefed to be spares. With no pilots aborting, they broke off from the formation before it reached the target area. However, instead of returning to base they made a low-level run over the Alps where, just for fun, they dropped their tanks and then strafed them to set them on fire. They then made a leisurely tour of the area around the Swiss-Italian-German border. This sightseeing trip meant they were the last to arrive home.

After hearing about the exploits of the rest of the group, Anderson's crew chief rushed to the aircraft, anxious to know how many his pilot had scored. 'None', croaked Anderson, who later admitted that when he learned he had missed out on a record mission 'I felt sick'.

——— SPARRING WITH THE *SCHWALBE*———

After 'Big Day' a mission to escort B-24s to the airfield at Leipheim on 15 January seemed tame. On the way home a member of Lt Robert Winks' flight spotted an aerodrome near Shongau. On it were parked 15 Me 262s, but because the airfield was well defended with deadly flak batteries, strafing was prohibited. Maj Richard Peterson was leading and he orbited the field so he could take photographs with the K-25 camera that he had brought with him specifically for this purpose.

While orbiting, Winks 'sighted an enemy aircraft doing a series of slow rolls on the deck. I went down from about 15,000 ft, got on his tail and fired a burst just as the enemy aircraft was approaching the aerodrome. I observed many strikes and the fuselage burst into flames. The enemy aircraft crashed on the edge of the field and blew up'. This single victory, which had made Winks an ace, came at the expense of trainee pilot Fahnrich Rudolf Rhodee.

As the Me 262 fell to earth, 'from some point behind me, probably not 50 ft away, I heard "Pete" Peterson say "Nice shooting!" He was right there, camera and all, just in case', said Winks. At that moment all the flak batteries surrounding Shongau opened up. Winks hauled his Mustang into a climb, converting the speed he had built up in his dive into altitude. Then his engine quit. He realised that when he had dropped his external tanks he had forgotten to move the fuel selector switch to internal fuel. Winks flipped the switch and the engine roared back to life, enabling him to make good his escape.

The group escorted B-17s to the marshalling yards at Bad Heilbrunn on 20 January. Afterwards the 364th was strafing trains when the pilots spotted two Me 262s near Braunschweig. 'It appeared one '262 pilot was checking out the other one in the jet', said Richard Peterson. The German fighters split up, one diving to 18,000 ft while the second climbed to 24,000 ft and began to circle around the Mustangs. 'It looked to me as if the upper jet was waiting for me to attack the lower one', Peterson explained.

He told Lt Dale Karger and White Flight to deal with the high-flying Me 262. They climbed to attack and the jet turned into them, coming at them head-on but not firing. Karger and wingman Lt Lloyd Zacharie reversed course and started chasing the jet, but the Me 262 pulled away and nearly disappeared into the distance. Then, possibly because the pilot thought he had had lost the Mustangs, he started a long left-hand turn.

On 15 February 1945 Capt Don Bochkay's P-51D-15 44-15422 suffered severe damage after a belly-landing at Leiston with Lt John Casey at the controls. The Mustang's engine had overheated during an extended period of taxiing and popped its coolant relief valve immediately after take-off (*Olmsted via Roeder*)

The P-51 pilots cut the corner and Karger fired a burst which struck the Me 262 near the cockpit. The enemy pilot bailed out and his jet did a neat split-s into the ground. This victory gave Karger ace status.

'When the upper '262 was eliminated, the remaining jet headed for home in a hurry', continued Peterson. He tried to dive on the jet, but before he could line up a shot the Me 262 sped away. Not to be dissuaded, Peterson led his remaining two flights to Lechfeld, where he thought the surviving jet would have to land. 'We were not sure which way the jet would approach the runway, so Lt Ernest Tiede and I cruised toward the south end. Lt Ed Haydon and Lt Roland Wright spotted him coming in from the north, however, so Lt Haydon went for the jet, but he was too high and made an easy target for the flak gunners.'

'I heard Maj Peterson tell Lt Haydon to hit the deck as light flak was coming up before he reached the field in his run', commented Lt Robert Schimanski. 'I heard someone say, "I'm on fire, I'm bailing out". Haydon quickly abandoned his blazing P-51D and floated safely down onto the airfield to become a PoW. Following right behind him after the Me 262 – but at a lower altitude – was Roland Wright. 'I continued on in, getting close to the deck, and saw numerous strikes on the cockpit and wing area of the enemy aircraft', stated Wright. 'I stayed on the deck, taking evasive action until I was away from the airfield, as the flak was thick all around me. After getting away I looked back and saw black smoke coming from the airfield. I believe that the Me 262 burned'.

Weather kept the number of missions to a minimum as January turned into February. Finally, on the 9th, the 357th FG again encountered the Luftwaffe during an escort mission for bombers targeting Bohleim. The 363rd FS mustered a spare flight that was led by Capt Browning and included Capt Don Bochkay, who reported;

'Around the Fulda area a gaggle of four Me 262s was called in about 4000 ft below us, headed for the bomber formation. We dropped tanks and Capt Browning dove to the left for attack. The four Me 262s broke up. Two dove to the right and two dove to the left. I climbed high, balls-out, keeping the Me 262s in

Capt Jim Browning and crew pose with P-51D-15 Mustang 44-14937 *GENTLEMAN JIM*, which other pilots said was an apt nickname for the genteel Kansan. The circumstances of Browning's loss – he collided with an Me 262 over the town of Woersdorf on 9 February 1945 – remained a mystery until 1947 (*Olmsted via Roeder*)

sight, as well as covering Capt Browning. I climbed to 28,000 ft and levelled off, at which point the two Me 262s broke right in a steep climbing turn. I dove my ship to gain more speed. The sun was in my favour and I believe the Me 262s did not see me. I passed under the lead Me 262 and broke hard to the right, coming out on the second Me 262's tail at 300 yards. I fired a long burst as he was pulling away from me but I observed some very good hits about the canopy and right engine. That really slowed him down. The lead Me 262 headed straight down.

'The one I hit broke to the left in a gentle turn, so I opened up on him again at about 400 yards and kept firing all the way in on him. I saw many strikes all over him and his canopy shattered, along with large pieces flying off the enemy aircraft. I broke off to the right to keep from running into him. As I passed very close to him the pilot was halfway out of his cockpit. The ship then rolled over on its back and the pilot fell out. He never opened his parachute and the aeroplane went straight on in. I then pulled up in a climbing left turn to rejoin Capt Browning, but we got separated because there were so many P-51s in the area with the same coloured tails.'

Unseen by Bochkay, Browning had headed after the Me 262 flown by Oberstleutant *Freiherr* von Riedsel, CO of KG(J) 54. Although no one in the air saw it, people in the town of Woersdorf witnessed Browning's Mustang converge on the jet, then collide with it. Both aircraft burst into flames and spun in, crashing 600 yards apart near the town's railway station. Browning was killed and Riedsel, who was severely wounded, died in hospital the next day.

Capt Chester Maxwell's P-51D-20 Mustang 44-63861 *Elixir!/Lady Esther* came to a sad end on 25 February 1945 when its engine failed and the ace crash-landed at East Wretham (*359th FG Association via Randall*)

Another view of Capt Maxwell's demolished *Elixir!/Lady Esther*. The pilot was unharmed and able to return to Leiston after this crash (*359th FG Association via Randall*)

Lt Johnnie Carter in Green Flight gave chase to a jet being vainly pursued by Lt Foy, but was outpaced by both the jet and the diving Mustang. As the fight drew away from him, he looked down and saw another Me 262 below, apparently without power. Carter split-ess'ed onto the jet's tail, opened fire and hit the Me 262. The pilot's canopy came off and the German pilot bailed out, giving Carter his fourth, and last, aerial victory.

Strafing missions were flown on 25 and 28 February, but the group had to wait until 2 March before it claimed its next aerial successes. Whilst escorting 'heavies' to Ruhland, Lt Col Joe Broadhead's flight spotted a dogfight in progress at 28,000 ft northeast of Leipzig. His squadron waded in and quickly downed three Bf 109s. Capt John Sublett had already shot down two fighters when a single Me 262 made an attack on a nearby B-24 formation. 'I immediately gave chase, my flight following me', he said. Sublett damaged the jet but it soon out-ran him.

The 363rd's Capt Donald McGee, who had 'made ace' in the Pacific theatre in 1942-43 flying P-38s and P-39s, added a solitary kill to his tally when he destroyed a Bf 109 – it was his unit's sole claim on 2 March. The 364th FS, however, was credited with 8.5 kills, Capt Alva Murphy leading the way with two Bf 109s to achieve 'acedom'. He was killed later in the mission, however, when his aircraft was downed by flak during a strafing attack southwest of Magdeburg. Squadronmate Capt Robert Schimanski also secured ace status with 1.5 victories, as did Lt Raymond Bank, who claimed a solitary Bf 109. Like Murphy, his fighter also succumbed to flak, although he survived bellying in behind enemy lines. Bank became a PoW. He was one of three pilots from the 357th to be captured on 2 March, with two more killed in action. All bar one of them had fallen to flak.

On 19 March the group provided an escort for bombers that were again sent to attack Ruhland. During the mission pilots encountered the largest force of Me 262s yet seen – 36 jets. 'They came in from "six o'clock high" in waves of 12, each wave consisting of four flights in "V" formation', reported Lt Col Andy Evans. 'Our 363rd FS, led by Lt Col Hayes, was able to prevent the last two waves from hitting the bombers. These jets went into a slight dive, breaking into two-ship elements that easily outdistanced our pursuit'.

Capt Alva Murphy poses in the cockpit of his fighter, which displays victory markings for four aerial and two strafing victories. As it happened, Murphy's final aerial score was six, as he accounted for two Bf 109s on 2 March 1945 before he was shot down and killed by flak while strafing an airfield (*Olmsted via Roeder*)

Three of the group's 'big wheels' at war's end, Lt Col Jack Hayes (left), who shot down an Me 262 and became CO of the 55th FG, Lt Col Andy Evans (centre), who claimed six kills, and Col Irwin Dregne, who downed five (*Olmsted via Roeder*)

Despite the group's efforts in downing one jet, the third wave of Me 262s shot down two B-17s of the 452nd BG and one each from the 96th and 385th BGs. About 20 minutes after the attack, as the group was heading home, Foy spotted three P-51s below him being stalked by four Me 262s. He reported;

'I turned left to cut them off, and at about 6000 ft the jets levelled off on a straight course. The jets apparently did not see our flight as we started to close on them. Suddenly, they appeared to pull away from us. Although I was still a bit out of range, I pulled the K-14 gunsight pip just a bit high of one of the jet aircraft and gave him two good short bursts just for good luck. I was frankly surprised to see the left engine nacelle of the jet start smoking a black trail. The jet immediately did a half roll to the left into a split-s. The jet continued its dive from 6000 ft into the ground, exploding in a cloud of flame and smoke just west of an airfield.'

The German pilot was probably Oberfeldwebel Heinz-Berthold Mattuschka of JG 7.

The next day's mission to Augsburg resulted in two claims, including one by ace Capt John Sublett, against conventionally powered fighters. But on the 21st the jets took their revenge during an escort mission to Ruhland when a large number of them attacked the American force, with at least five bombers shot down ahead of the section of the stream covered by the 357th.

Six missions were squeezed into the next three days, although enemy aircraft were only encountered on the 24th. The 364th FS was prowling the area west of Gutersloh when its pilots sighted bandits airborne over the aerodrome. 'We made a 180-degree turn and dove on their tails', reported Capt Paul Hatala. 'The enemy aircraft saw us and broke up to fight. I picked out an Me 109 and started turning with him. I got strikes in the wing. Pieces came off and it went into a dive from 3000 ft. The pilot bailed out and his 'chute opened.

'I looked at my tail and saw another '109 firing away at very close range. I immediately went into a steep turn to the right and dropped flaps. The '109 couldn't stay with me, so he dropped out. When I levelled out he came in on me so he was set up for a 90-degree deflection shot. I got good hits on his wings and in the cockpit. Hits in his right wing

SSgt Art Krantz poses with Lt Dale Karger's second Mustang, P-51D-20 44-72313 *Cathy Mae II*. The aircraft displays eight kill markings on the canopy rail, although the 19-year-old ace's final score was 7.5 aerial and four strafing victories (*Olmsted via Roeder*)

The port side of Col Irwin Dregne's P-51K-5 44-11678 *BOBBY JEANNE/Ah Fung-Goo* shows off his scoreboard. Note the AN/APS-13 tail warning radar antenna on the vertical fin. More than 20 of the group's Mustangs featured this additional equipment by the war's end (*Olmsted via Roeder*)

knocked part of the wing off and he dished out and dove for the ground at about an 80-degree angle'.

Hatala then noticed a Bf 109 on the tail of a P-51. 'I got on the tail of this enemy aircraft and started shooting. I got some strikes on the wing and fuselage. He then levelled out and I gave him another burst. Pieces came off the enemy aircraft and the pilot bailed out'. The latter victory gave Paul Hatala the distinction of being the very last pilot from the 357th FG to attain ace status.

Capt Robert Schimanski was leading White Flight when he spotted a gaggle of Bf 109s below him. He quickly positioned his flight for a bounce. 'I picked out one for myself, put the pipper on him and waited for him to blow up. But I couldn't wait long enough to put the finishing touches on him', Schimanski recalled. 'I started turning with another Me 109, finally catching him on the top of a climbing turn. I hit him in the cockpit and he snapped on his back and tumbled into the ground from about 2000 ft'. Seven more German aircraft fell to the 364th that day, with aces Lt Col John Storch and Lt Dale Karger being among the victors, as was Lt Col Andy Evans of the HQ flight.

The 362nd pilots had heard the radio chatter from the 364th and headed for the action. 'The fight was at "12 o'clock low" and we immediately started towards the engagement', said Capt Charles Weaver. He entered into a Lufbery, but lost the advantage and dove away. Weaver reported;

'Finally, I singled out a lone Jerry making haste from the scene of the action. I turned and gave chase. My first burst, of three seconds, was at 650-700 yards. I observed strikes on the nose and engine cowling. The Me 109 pulled up in a chandelle to the left and I closed very rapidly, firing a long second burst at 200 yards, noting strikes on the nose, engine, cockpit and all other parts of the enemy aircraft. Pieces were flying thick and fast. The pilot jettisoned his canopy and tried with some difficulty to get out. I gave several short bursts at 50-70 yards, at which point the pilot popped out of his cockpit. The Jerry's 'chute did not open until he was about 80 ft from the ground. It did not have time to blossom.'

The squadron hacked down two more enemy fighters.

The 363rd was flying its own segment of the sweep not far away when pilots heard about the hunting around Gutersloh. Maj Robert Foy soon spotted two Bf 109s hugging the deck;

'I alerted the squadron and started to dive onto the tail of the enemy aircraft. They apparently saw us diving to attack and one enemy aircraft on the right side of the two-ship formation broke right and I lost sight

Maj Bob Foy completed two tours with the 357th FG and finished the war with 15 aerial and three strafing victories to his name. He perished in a flying accident involving a B-25 on 25 March 1950 while working for North American Aviation (*Olmsted via Roeder*)

of him. The lead ship broke left and I continued onto his tail, pulling into range, giving him a short burst. He obligingly straightened out at about 600 ft. I closed in rapidly, giving him more short bursts. The last burst clobbered him squarely and he began streaming smoke. He headed toward the deck and made a feeble attempt to crash land. He hit upon his right wing and cartwheeled, tearing the aeroplane to bits.'

Foy circled and saw the German pilot running from the crash. He strafed the pilot and killed him, but when he tried to pull up he hit a tree with his left wing, then bounced off a second with his right wing. Foy somehow managed to fly his battered Mustang home.

The day was marred by the death of 8.5-kill ace Lt Otto Jenkins. After completing the mission, which was the last of his tour, the Texan decided to beat up the field at Leiston but crashed in the process.

Luftwaffe fighters were now becoming difficult to find in the air over Germany, and it was not until 7 April that the 357th added to its burgeoning tally of aerial victories with two Bf 109s destroyed. Neither fell to aces, however. Three days later the group escorted bombers to Neuruppin, then strafed an airfield near the target. Its pilots destroyed some 23 enemy aircraft without suffering any loss, Col Dregne claiming two Me 262s destroyed and Lt Col Evans an He 111 and an Me 210.

More strafing successes came on 16 and 17 April, and an Me 262 was also credited to Flt Off James Steiger of the 364th FS. Attacks on

Lt Otto Jenkins lines up P-51D-20 44-63199 *TOOLIN' FOOL'S REVENGE* for take-off from Leiston in February 1945. On 24 March the 8.5-victory ace was killed when this aircraft clipped trees and crashed at Leiston during a low-level flypast to mark the end of his operational tour (*Olmsted via Roeder*)

Prague-Ruzyne dominated during this period, as the USAAF had determined that retreating Luftwaffe units in the east had converged on this airfield, and others nearby. Indeed, Col Dregne reported sighting 200 aircraft at the aerodrome on 17 April. Lts John Duncan and Anton Schoepke of the 362nd shot up two Me 262s on this date, leaving them burning, but strafing was not undertaken without cost.

'We ran into severe flak', said Lt Osborn Howes. 'Lt Irving Snedeker was on my wing. He fell behind me as we approached the field'. Suddenly, Snedeker's aircraft was hit by a shell that tore away its propeller. The Mustang mushed in on the field and broke in two behind the cockpit. Snedeker scrambled from the wreck and sat down, lit a cigarette and waited for the Germans to capture him. Lts Robert Muller and James Monahan were also knocked down by flak, and all three pilots became PoWs.

Recognising the threat posed by the Me 262s, the Eighth Air Force had briefed the 357th FG to cover the airfields near Prague an hour before the arrival of the bombers on 18 April. Since the Me 262s had limited endurance, the plan was to either knock them out as they took off or strafe them on the ground. Maj 'Kit' Carson led the mission. Through some superb navigation the group was able to fly a zigzag course at low altitude to disguise its intentions. It hit Prague-Ruzyne at exactly 1300 hrs, at which point Carson despatched Maj Don Bochkay to cover the two nearby fields, then orbited Prague-Ruzyne to see what the German fighter pilots would do. Soon, the Mustang pilots saw the jets taxi out for take-off. Carson wrote later;

'As the first '262 started his take-off roll we dropped our wing tanks and I started down with Red Flight from 13,000 ft with an easy wing-over. The '262 pilot had his gear up and was going past the field boundary when we ploughed through intense light flak. As I came astern of him and levelled off at 400+ mph, I firewalled it to hold my speed

Capt Tom Adams' P-51D-20 Mustang 44-64099 *ARKANSAS TRAVELLER* survived the war to have buzz numbers painted under the wing. Adams, who claimed 4.5 aerial and one strafing victories, scored two kills on 'Big Day' in this aircraft (*Olmsted via Roeder*)

Maj Don Bochkay strikes a jaunty pose with his final aircraft, P-51D-20 44-72244, which lacks shrouds on the exhausts – a common field modification made to the 357th's Mustangs. Bochkay ended the war with 13.833 victories, the last of which (an Me 262) was claimed in this aircraft on 18 April 1945 (*Olmsted via Roeder*)

and centred the bull's eye of the optical sight on the fuselage and hit him with a two-second burst.'

Carson's timing was slightly off, for although he scored strikes he only claimed the jet as damaged. Capt 'Chuck' Weaver, however, caught an Me 262 trying to land and shot it down, the wreckage landing on the field. He and Lt Oscar Ridley had both gone after the Me 262 as it drew the Mustangs across the airfield. This resulted in them being targeted by 'considerable flak', related Weaver. 'Lt Ridley called that he had been hit. I returned to the field and told him to fly west for as long as possible. I caught up with him at a point 20 miles west of Prague. His engine was smoking badly. He said the fire was bad and he was leaving the aeroplane. He bailed out at 5000 ft. His 'chute opened successfully'. Ridley was the last pilot to be lost by the group as a result of enemy action.

Bochkay, meanwhile, was leading the 363rd's Blue Flight when he heard White Flight call in a bogey at '11 o'clock low'. The ace recalled;

'I recognised it as an Me 262. I dropped my tanks and dove, pulling up behind the jet. I then let him have a burst from 400 yards, getting very good hits on his right jet unit and canopy. He then broke right in a very

Another view of Maj Don Bochkay's final mount, 44-72244, at rest at Leiston soon after the war in Europe had come to an end. This photograph represents something of an enigma because it depicts the aircraft without Bochkay's personal winged ace of clubs emblem on the nose. The fighter eventually went into storage at Speke (*Kyburz via Randall*)

What the Luftwaffe could not achieve the wreckers' did. Maj 'Kit' Carson's P-51K-5 44-11622 *Nooky Booky IV,* still displaying its pilot's final scoreboard, languishes in a scrap yard in Neubiberg, Germany, in 1946. The hole in the national insignia represents the location of the foul-weather formation light – an addition intended to make forming up in English weather less hazardous (*Olmsted via Roeder*)

tight diving turn, pulling streamers from his wingtips. As he straightened out at 7000 ft I let him have another burst, getting very good hits on his right jet unit again. He then popped his canopy as I let him have another burst. Large pieces came off his ship and it caught fire. I pulled off to miss the pieces and watched the Me 262 fall apart. His tail came off. It then rolled over and went in like a torch, crashing into some woods next to a river. The pilot never got out.'

It was Maj Don Bochkay's second Me 262 kill, and the last aerial victory credited to an ace from the 357th FG.

Lt Col Jack Hayes led the group to Prague-Ruzyne ahead of the bombers once again on the 20th, effectively clamping a lid on the jet base. Again, almost fatalistically, the Me 262s started taking off in pairs, hoping to evade the Mustangs. Hayes' flight bounced two of them. Hayes himself got strikes on the element leader, who turned left, headed for the deck at full power and shrieked across the Danube. The Me 262 went behind a tower on the eastern bank of the river, and as Hayes cleared the tower he was rewarded with the sight of the Me 262 crashing, its flaming wreckage sliding into a building. The group succeeded in destroying four more Me 262s during the mission.

On 25 April four aircraft were sent out as an escort for air-sea rescue efforts, shepherding a Warwick and a Catalina in a fruitless search for downed airmen. Little did the pilots know that this would be their final mission. With the end of the war in Europe, the official order came from Eighth Air Force Command on 8 May to stand down from operations. A flypast over London on the 13th and participation in a parade three days later proved to be the highlights of the group's immediate post-war period.

On 14 June the 357th FG was ordered to Germany for occupation duty. A month later, Leiston saw the last of the 'Yoxford Boys', and by 31 July the group was back in business at Neubiberg. Andy Evans relieved Irwin Dregne, but his command was shrinking rapidly. In October alone, 300 pilots and crewmen departed for the US. By then only 15 Mustangs were flyable, and all three squadrons were consolidated into the 362nd FS. By December, five Mustangs were left airworthy and in August of 1946 the group was finally stricken from the rolls of active USAAF units.

Despite its relatively short existence, the 357th FG had been a spectacular success. Indeed, during its time in combat the group had scored 595.5 aerial victories and produced 42 aces.

APPENDICES

Aces of the 357th Fighter Group

Ranking	Name	Unit(s)	Final Score (aerial victories only)
1	Maj Leonard K 'Kit' Carson	362nd FS	18.5 (11 Fw 190s, 6.5 Bf 109s, 1 Me 410)
2	Maj John B England	362nd FS	17.5 (8.5 Bf 109s, 5 Fw 190s, 4 Bf 110s)
3	Capt Clarence E 'Bud' Anderson Jr	363rd FS	16.25 (9 Fw 190s, 7 Bf 109s, 0.25 He 111)
4	Capt Richard A 'Pete' Peterson	364th FS	15.5 (8 Bf 109s, 5.5 Fw 190s, 1.5 Me 410s, 0.5 Bf 110)
5	Maj Robert W Foy	363rd FS/357th FG	15 (8 Bf 109s, 4 Fw 190s, 2 Ju 88s, 1 Me 262)
6	Maj Donald H Bochkay	363rd FS	13.833 (5.5 Bf 109s, 4.333 Fw 190s, 2 Me 262s, 2 Bf 110s)
7	Lt John A Kirla	362nd FS	11.5 (6 Fw 190s, 5.5 Bf 109s)
7	Capt Charles E 'Chuck' Yeager	363rd FS	11.5 (6.5 Bf 109s, 4 Fw 190s, 1 Me 262)
9	Lt Col John A Storch	364th FS	10.5 (7.5 Bf 109s, 3 Fw 190s)
10	Capt Fletcher E Adams (KIA)	362nd FS	9 (4.5 Bf 109s, 3 Bf 110s, 1 Fw 190, 0.5 Me 410)
11	Lt Col Thomas L Hayes Jr	364th FS/357th FG	8.5 (6 Bf 109s, 1.5 Me 410s, 1 Bf 110)
11	Lt Otto D Jenkins (KIFA)	362nd FS	8.5 (6 Fw 190s, 2.5 Bf 109s)
13	Maj Joseph E Broadhead	362nd FS	8 (4 Bf 109s, 3 Fw 190s, 1 Bf 110)
13	Lt Robert M Shaw	364th FS	8 (5 Bf 109s, 2 Fw 190s, 1 Me 410)
13	Capt John L Sublett	362nd FS	8 (4 Bf 109s, 4 Fw 190s)
13	Capt Charles E Weaver	362nd FS	8 (4 Bf 109s, 3 Fw 190s, 1 Me 262)
17	Lt Dale E Karger	364th FS	7.5 (4.5 Bf 109s, 2 Fw 190s, 1 Me 262)
17	Capt Glendon V Davis	364th FS	7.5 (2 Fw 200s, 2 Fw 190s, 2 Bf 109s, 1.5 Bf 110s)
19	Capt Robert H Becker	362nd FS	7 (4.5 Bf 109s, 1.5 Bf 110s, 1 Fw 190)
19	Capt James W Browning (KIA)	363rd FS	7 (5 Bf 109s, 1.5 Me 410s, 0.5 Fw 190)
19	Lt John B Carder (PoW)	364th FS	7 (6 Bf 109s, 1 Fw 190)
19	Lt Gilbert M O'Brien	362nd FS	7 (3.5 Bf 109s, 3 Fw 190s, 0.5 Me 410)
19	Lt Joseph E Pierce (KIA)	363rd FS	7 (3 Fw 190s, 2 Bf 109s, 1 Ju 88, 1 Bf 110)
19	Lt Gerald E Tyler	364th FS	7 (5 Bf 109s, 2 Fw 190s)
25	Lt Col Andrew J Evans Jr	357th FG	6 (5 Fw 190s, 1 Bf 109)
25	Capt Alva C Murphy (KIA)	362nd FS/364th FS	6 (5 Bf 109s, 1 Fw 190)
25	Capt John F Pugh	362nd FS	6 (4 Bf 109s, 2 Fw 190s)
25	Lt Arval J Roberson	362nd FS	6 (5.5 Bf 109s, 0.5 Bf 110)
25	Capt Robert G Schimanski	364th FS	6 (5 Bf 109s, 1 Fw 190)
30	Lt Frank L Gailer (PoW)	363rd FS	5.5 (3.5 Fw 190s, 2 Bf 109s)
30	Capt Paul R Hatala	364th FS	5.5 (3.5 Bf 109s, 2 Fw 190s)
30	Capt William R O'Brien	363rd FS	5.5 (5 Bf 109s, 0.5 Bf 110)
30	Lt LeRoy A Ruder (KIA)	364th FS	5.5 (2 Bf 109s, 2 Fw 109s, 1.5 Bf 110s)
30	Lt Robert P Winks	364th FS	5.5 (3 Fw 190s, 1.5 Bf 109s, 1 Me 262)
35	Maj Raymond M Bank (PoW)	364th FS	5 (3 Fw 190s, 2 Bf 109s)
35	Lt Col Irwin H Dregne	357th FG	5 (5 Bf 109s)
35	Lt Thomas L Harris	364th FS	5 (2 Bf 109s, 2 Fw 190s, 1 Bf 110)
35	Maj Edwin W Hiro (KIA)	363rd FS	5 (5 Bf 109s)
35	Capt Chester K Maxwell	364th FS	5 (4 Fw 190s, 1 Bf 109)
35	Lt William C Reese (KIA)	364th FS	5 (3 Bf 109s, 1 Bf 110, 1 Do 217)
35	Lt Morris A Stanley	364th FS	5 (3 Fw 190s, 1 Me 410, 1 Fw 200)
35	Capt Jack R Warren (KIA)	364th FS	5 (2 Fw 190s, 2 Bf 110s, 1 Bf 109)

Key

KIA – killed in action

KIFA – killed in flying accident

PoW – prisoner of war

1

P-51B-5 43-6653 LI'L RED'S ROCKET of Lt Thomas Harris, 364th FS, Leiston, March 1944

Thomas Harris destroyed two Bf 109s during a mission to Ludwigshafen on 27 May 1944, making him an ace, but he was unable to enjoy this distinction. While flying this aircraft, 'Li'l Red' Harris collided with the P-51C (42-106632) flown by squadronmate Lt Dean Post and he became a prisoner of war before he could report his success. Post was killed. This aircraft features the original white nose, wing and fin stripes worn by all Eighth Air Force fighters prior to the introduction of group markings.

2

P-51B-10 42-106447 SHOO SHOO BABY of Lt John Howell, 364th FS, Leiston, March 1944

John Howell scored two and one shared victories, the most notable of which was over 92-kill ace Gerhard Loos of JG 54 on 6 March 1944. On 21 May Howell was flying this aircraft (fitted with a coveted Malcolm hood) during a sweep when he and wingman Lt Bill Reese attacked a flak train. Reese, a five-kill ace, was shot down and Howell's aircraft sustained a holed vertical fin. A second firing pass mangled the Mustang's wingtip but, using trim tabs and throttle, Howell brought the aircraft home safely. He remained in the USAF post-war and served in the Berlin Airlift, Korea and Vietnam, before retiring as a lieutenant colonel. Having survived for more than a year with the 364th FS, 42-106447 was lost in a mid-air collision with P-51B 43-24766 during a training mission on 27 February 1945 that cost the lives of rookie pilots Lts Ralph E Eisert and Robert R Hoffman. Neither man had flown a mission prior to their deaths.

3

P-51B-5 43-6878 Pregnant Polecat of Capt Glendon Davis, 364th FS, Leiston, April 1944

Glen Davis graduated from flight training in mid-1942 and became one of the 364th FS's first pilots. He enjoyed a brief but successful career that resulted in him claiming 5.5 victories between 5 and 16 March 1944 to become the group's first ace. His scoring opened with two Fw 200s shot down on 5 March, followed by a Bf 110 and an Fw 190 shared with Tom Harris the next day. On 8 March Davis shared a Bf 109 with Harris, then became an ace eight days later when he shot down a Bf 109 and shared in the destruction of a Bf 110. He added single fighters to his score on 13 and 19 April, but the engine of Pregnant Polecat failed over France on 28 April. Davis bailed out but avoided capture, and he eventually returned to England in September.

4

P-51B-5 43-6935 Hurry Home Honey of Capt Richard Peterson, 364th FS, Leiston, May 1944

The first of three identically named Mustangs, 'Pete' Peterson's mount was inspired by the sign-off his wife used on all her letters. Peterson, who hailed from Alexandria, Minnesota, flew 150 missions and served with the group from its time at Tonopah until the end of the war. He

developed a reputation for looking after newcomers, and at the same time was able to score 15.5 victories. After the war Peterson returned to Minnesota and became a noted architect. 43-6935 was lost on 20 June 1944 when it was hit by flak north of Paris. Its pilot, Lt Heyward C Spinks, successfully evaded.

5

P-51B-15 42-106826 THE SHILLELAGH of Capt John Storch, 362nd FS, Leiston, May 1944

John Storch suffered a broken arm which grounded him during the group's first few combat missions, and it was not until 12 May that he opened his score when he shared in the destruction of an Fw 190 with 'Pete' Peterson. This particular aircraft was the first of three SHILLELAGHs, although it was the only B-model. Fitted with a Malcolm hood, the fighter was used by Storch to claim four victories between 19 May and 20 June. Eventually transferred to Lt Nick Frederick and renamed Marie, the fighter was damaged in a landing accident at Leiston on 11 November. Having been repaired, 42-106826 was transferred to the 78th FG and converted into a two-seater 'hack' – it was given an overall red paint scheme for this role.

6

P-51D-5 44-13316 MILDRED of Capt Leonard Carson, 362nd FS, Leiston, June 1944

One of the first D-model Mustangs to arrive in England, on 4 June 1944, this aircraft was rushed to the 357th FG in time to receive full invasion stripes. Also applied to the aircraft was a nickname, the source of which neither 'Kit' Carson nor his crew chief could identify. It flew a few missions as MILDRED but was soon re-christened the more familiar Nooky Booky II. Carson flew this machine through to the late autumn, when it was transferred to Lt Ted Conlin to become Olivia de H. Its final fate is unknown.

7

P-51C-1 42-103309 BERLIN EXPRESS of Capt Bill Overstreet, 363rd FS, Leiston, June 1944

Virginia-born Bill Overstreet is perhaps best known for chasing a Bf 109 down Paris' Champs Elysees in this very machine on 29 June 1944. He even followed it under the arches of the Eiffel Tower before catching it and shooting it down. Overstreet failed to become ace, however, scoring 2.25 aerial and two strafing victories, but he flew more than 100 missions prior to being transferred home in October 1944. The fate of 42-103309 is also unknown.

8

P-51B-10 42-106462 U'VE HAD IT! of Capt John England, 362nd FS, Leiston, June 1944

John England's second Mustang (the first, P-51B-1 43-12462, had been a hand-me-down from the 354th FG), this aircraft was transferred to the 357th in March 1944 and soon received the characteristic 'half' paint scheme when the Olive Drab on the lower fuselage was stripped off. England claimed 2.5 victories in this aircraft prior to it being passed on to another pilot in July. The following month RAF exchange pilot Flt Lt Eric Wooley flew it on the shuttle mission to Russia. On 4 October the aircraft lost its tail assembly during a training flight, but its pilot, Lt Richard Potter, managed to bail out safely.

9

P-51D-5 44-13586 *Hurry Home Honey* of Capt Richard Peterson, 364th FS, Leiston, July 1944

On 1 July 1944, 'Pete' Peterson was flying the second *Hurry Home Honey* while escorting B-17s from the 91st BG. According to a radio operator aboard one of the Flying Fortresses, upon sighting enemy fighters Peterson radioed, 'I'll be right back, fellas – I'm gonna go play with these boys'. The result was two Bf 109s destroyed, giving Peterson his 10th and 11th victories. This aircraft was eventually passed on to Lt Horace Howell and was re-named *Flak Happy*, before being issued to Lt George Kouris. Inspired by his Greek parentage, the latter nicknamed it *Greece Lightning*. Kouris was forced to bail out of 44-13586 on 3 February 1945 after suffering mechanical failure southwest of Brunswick. He spent the rest of the war as a PoW.

10

P-51D-5 44-13517 *Sebastian Jr* of Capt Robert Becker, 362nd FS, Leiston, July 1944

Robert Becker scored seven victories and might have achieved an eighth but for German confusion on 25 July 1944. He was chasing an Fw 190 at low altitude over Paris in this aircraft when his victim suddenly dropped its nose and slammed into the ground, the apparent victim of 'friendly fire'. Ultimately, Becker used this aircraft to claim just a share in a Bf 109 on 29 July (he completed his tour early the following month), all 6.5 of his previous kills being scored in P-51Bs. 44-13517 was the second Mustang to be called *Sebastian*, the first one being P-51B-15 42-106783.

11

P-51D-5 44-13678 of Lt Morris Stanley, 364th FS, Leiston, July 1944

Morris Stanley achieved ace status when he downed two enemy fighters over Ludwigshafen on 27 May 1944. On 19 April he had shot down an Fw 190, firing just 60 rounds at the enemy fighter. When his quarry attempted a turn at low altitude, its pilot lost control and hit the ground. 'The Fw 190 must not be able to turn steeply to the right', Stanley reported. Although this aircraft remained nondescript throughout Stanley's five-victory tour, it was later named *Million Dollar Baby* and then *Linda J*. The fighter's final fate remains unrecorded.

12

P-51B-5 43-6787 *SHANTY IRISH* of Lt Gilbert O'Brien, 362nd FS, Leiston, July 1944

A native of Charleston, South Carolina, Gilbert O'Brien achieved seven kills, scoring the fifth to 'make ace' during a mission (on 30 May) in which his wingman, and fellow ace, Lt Fletcher Adams was shot down and later killed by his captors. O'Brien's last victory came on 29 July near Merseburg when he bounced a Bf 109 in a borrowed P-51D. After O'Brien's departure in August, this aircraft became

James Kenney's *Little Feetie* and, following a ground accident, it was converted into a two-seater called *Eager Beaver*.

13

P-51D-5 44-13318 *Frenesi* of Lt Col Tommy Hayes, 357th FG, Leiston, late July 1944

Born and raised in Portland, Oregon, Tommy Hayes was the original commander of the 364th FS. He brought experience to the new unit as he had fought the Japanese in Java in early 1942 until he was shot down and wounded. He later claimed two strafing victories in New Guinea after recovering from his injuries. This Mustang, *Frenesi* (pronounced *FREN-es-SEE*, and not *free 'n' easy* as some contend) was named after a popular song title at the time. 44-13318 was the third of four such aircraft assigned to Hayes that carried this name, and it was the only D-model Mustang to fly operationally with the group on D-Day. Hayes claimed 2.5 kills in the P-51D-5, although it is uncertain whether they were all in this machine. 44-13318 survived until 15 January 1945, when it was salvaged after suffering damage on 'Big Day'.

14

P-51D-5 44-13691 *Passion WAGON* of Lt Arval Roberson, 362nd FS, Leiston, September 1944

Arval Roberson flew his second *Passion WAGON* (his first was P-51B-5 43-6688) on the 19 September 1944 mission to cover the Operation *Market Garden* landings, during which he scored two Bf 109 kills and attained ace status. 'Although I named it, I told my mother the crew chief had, and he told his wife that he had nothing to do with it!', Roberson later said. He flew 76 missions in the Mustang in World War 2 and 100 more in the F-51 during the Korean War, plus a further 26 in C-47s during the Vietnam conflict while serving in a joint command position with the South Vietnamese air force. He retired from the USAF as a colonel in 1973. Once Roberson had completed his tour with the 362nd FS in late September 1944, this aircraft was passed on to future eight-kill ace Lt Charles Weaver. Its ultimate fate is unknown.

15

P-51D-5 44-13388 *BODACIOUS* of Col Donald Graham, CO of the 357th FG, Leiston, September 1944

Don Graham led the 357th FG between 7 March and 11 October 1944, his last major combat being fought over Holland during Operation *Market Garden*. Claiming a solitary aerial kill the day after he took command of the group, Graham's biggest contribution to the war effort may have come when he ordered a K-14 gyroscopic gunsight to be installed in *BODACIOUS*. This was copied by other Eighth Air Force units and eventually became the official method for retrofitting older P-51D Mustangs. Following Graham's departure, 44-13388 was flown by Lt William J Currie as *Super X* and by Lt Peter Pielich as *Peter Beater*. The latter pilot wrote the aircraft off in a crash-landing at Leiston on 3 April 1945.

16

P-51C-1 42-103002 *JEESIL PEESIL MOMMY* of Lt Frank Gailer, 363rd FS, Leiston, September 1944

Frank Gailer named his Mustang after his flight school roommate's pet expression for his wife. He claimed three shared kills while flying this fighter before ground looping it on 26 September 1944. 42-103002 was condemned for scrapping on 1 October. Gailer achieved ace status in P-51D-5 44-11331 on 27 November when he shot the wing clean off an Fw 190, causing the wildly gyrating fighter to collide with its wingman. Minutes later he was mistakenly shot down by Mustangs from the 352nd FG and spent the rest of the war as a PoW.

17
P-51D-10 44-14450 *OLD CROW* of Capt 'Bud' Anderson, 363rd FS, Leiston, October 1944

Oakland, California-born 'Bud' Anderson started his series of aircraft called *OLD CROW* with a P-39 during training in his home state. This was the third Mustang to bear the name, and it displays 13 kill markings, representing 12.25 victories – he had shared in the destruction of an He 111 with three other pilots on 11 April 1944. This machine flew in its field-applied camouflage until the autumn of 1944, when it was stripped back to bare metal overnight by Anderson's dedicated groundcrew. 44-14450 was subsequently passed on to Lt James Taylor (who renamed it *Pretty Pix*) following the completion of Anderson's tour, and on 14 January he claimed his solitary aerial victory in it.

18
P-51D-10 44-14660 *LITTLE DUCKFOOT* of Lt Gerald Tyler, 364th FS, Leiston, October 1944

Gerald Tyler scored a triple kill while flying this aircraft, his second *LITTLE DUCKFOOT* (the first was P-51B-5 43-6376), over Arnhem on 18 September during Operation *Market Garden*, destroying two Bf 109s and an Fw 190. These successes gave him ace status, and he claimed his seventh, and last, kill (another Bf 109) in the same area the following day. 44-14660 was written off in a taxiing accident at Leiston on 19 October 1944. Tyler remained in the USAF post-war and retired with the rank of lieutenant colonel. His relationship with the Mustang did not end there, for in the 1960s he was General Manager and Vice President of Cavalier Aircraft Corporation, which rebuilt P-51s for civilian and military use. In 1968 he flew one of his company's aircraft non-stop across the Atlantic.

19
P-51D-15 44-14888 *GLAMOROUS GLEN III* of Capt 'Chuck' Yeager, 363rd FS, Leiston, November 1944

'Chuck' Yeager was flying his third *GLAMOROUS GLEN* when he destroyed four Fw 190s southwest of Magdeburg on 27 November 1944. The West Virginian enlisted in the US Army Air Corps in September 1941 at a time when flight training requirements stipulated a college degree, which Yeager lacked. Wartime alterations to the criteria allowed him to enter flight training in March 1943, and Yeager joined the 357th as an original member of the unit. He was shot down in the original and mis-spelled (to American eyes) *GLAMOURUS GLEN* (P-51B-7 43-6763) on 5 March 1944, but evaded both the Germans and USAAF policy to return to combat flying with the group. 44-14888 became *Melody's Answer* after Yeager completed his tour in January 1945, and it was lost to flak over Haseloff on 2 March. Its pilot, Flt Off Patrick L Mallione, perished.

20
P-51D-10 44-14245 *FLOOGIE II* of Lt Otto Jenkins, 362nd FS, Leiston, December 1944

Otto Jenkins, who hailed from Kermit, Texas, scored most of his successes while flying this Mustang, and it was with this fighter that he destroyed four Fw 190s on Christmas Eve 1944. Like 'Chuck' Yeager, 'Dittie' Jenkins came to the group as a flight officer but was soon promoted to lieutenant. His final score was 8.5 victories. On 13 January 1945, Lt Robert Schlieker became disoriented in bad weather when returning to Leiston in bad weather at the end of a mission and crashed *FLOOGIE II* south of the airfield near Woodbridge, wrecking the aircraft and losing his life.

21
P-51D-10 44-14625 *SPOOK* of Lt John Kirla, 362nd FS, Leiston, January 1945

New York-born John Kirla was the only double or triple ace in the 357th FG not to come from the group's original cadre of pilots. He was working in a Connecticut boat yard when war broke out and was drafted, initially going to an artillery unit before transferring to the USAAF. Kirla arrived in Leiston in May 1944, but it was not until 13 September that he opened his score with a kill and a shared victory with Otto Jenkins. 19 September was his only single-kill day – he destroyed a Bf 109 and an Fw 190 on 5 December (his first victories in this aircraft), three Fw 190s on Christmas Eve and two more Fw 190s and a pair of Bf 109s on 14 January. The latter four successes were claimed in P-51D-20 44-72180. 44-14625 was subsequently transferred to the 359th FG's 369th FS in early 1945.

22
P-51D-10 44-14798 *Master Mike* of Maj Joseph Broadhead, 357th FG, Leiston, January 1945

Eight-kill ace Joe Broadhead commanded the 362nd FS from 25 March until 28 August 1944, then returned to Leiston in October as group Operations Officer. A three-tour veteran who was described by other members of the 362nd as a 'rough pilot', he never enjoyed a multiple-victory day but instead achieved a sequence of single kills between 25 February 1944 and 14 January 1945. *Master Mike* replaced his P-51B-1 43-12227 *Baby Mike* when he returned to the ETO in October 1944, and it survived through to the end of the war. After Broadhead was repatriated in February 1945, the fighter was passed on to Lt Julian H Bertram, who renamed it *Butch Baby*. Immediately post-war 44-14798 was stripped of its Olive Drab paint and renamed *Dainty Dotty* by pilot Lt James C McLane.

23
P-51D-20 44-63861 *Elixir!/Lady Esther* of Capt Chester Maxwell, 364th FS, Leiston, January 1945

Chester Maxwell, an Oklahoman, scored three Fw 190 kills on 'Big Day' to become an ace while flying a P-51D-5. He was then attacked by Mustangs from another group and had to make a forced landing at Antwerp. Little more than a month later, on 25 February, the engine of his newly-assigned *Elixir!/Lady Esther* (latter name applied to the starboard side only) failed and Maxwell made an emergency landing at East Wretham, writing off yet another Mustang.

24

P-51D-25 44-15266 *FIRE BALL* of Lt Raymond Bank, 364th FS, Leiston, January 1945

Raymond Bank had a single claim to his credit before 'Big Day' on 14 January 1945, when he sent three Fw 190s to destruction. He became an ace on 2 March, but on the very same mission *FIRE BALL's* engine was hit by flak and Bank had to belly it in near Ruhland. Quickly captured, he spent the final two months of the war as a PoW.

25

P-51K-5 44-11622 *Nooky Booky IV* of Maj Leonard Carson, 362nd FS, Leiston, February 1945

'Kit' Carson enlisted in the USAAF from the University of Iowa and went on to become the 357th FG's leading ace with 18.5 aerial victories. The last of Carson's P-51s was this K-model, named *Nooky Booky* like his three previous mounts. Carson used it to destroy an Fw 190 on 24 December 1944 and two Fw 190s and a Bf 109 on 14 January 1945. He also damaged two Me 262s with it on 18 April. *Nooky Booky IV* was scrapped at Neubiberg, in Germany, in 1946.

26

P-51D-20 44-72313 *Cathy Mae II* of Lt Dale Karger, 364th FS, Leiston, February 1945

At 19 Dale Karger was the group's youngest ace, and he scored his first four victories in P-51D-15 44-15026 *Cathy Mae/KARGER'S DOLLIE* – the latter name was displayed on the right side of the nose. This aircraft was lost to flak over Paderborn on 10 January 1945, killing pilot Lt Fred C McCall. As a result, Karger was flying his new Mustang when he scored a kill on 'Big Day' and downed an Me 262 on 20 January to become an ace. Karger's final tally was 7.5 aerial and four strafing victories. The final fate of 44-72313 remains unrecorded.

27

P-51D-20 44-63621 *LITTLE SHRIMP* of Maj Robert Foy, 357th FG, Leiston, March 1945

New Yorker Robert Foy scored seven kills during his first combat tour followed by eight more on his second. The final five victories came at the controls of this machine, with two Fw 190s being destroyed on 'Big Day', and an Me 262 from JG 7 on 19 March and a Bf 109 five days later. Foy, who initially served with the 363rd FS, was the 357th HQ flight's highest scoring ace. Both he and this Mustang survived the war, but Foy was killed when the B-25 that he was flying for North American Aviation exploded in mid-air near Phoenix, Arizona, on 25 March 1950.

28

P-51D-20 44-64051 *"LITTLE SWEETIE 4"/She's My Gal* of Lt Col Andrew Evans, 357th FG, Leiston, March 1945

'Andy' Evans, a 1941 West Point graduate, served with fighter squadrons in the US and Iceland before being posted to the 357th FG's HQ flight in the autumn of 1944. Flying his first mission in the ETO on his 26th birthday (11 November 1944), he was credited with a single Fw 190 kill 16 days later, four Fw 190s on 'Big Day' and a Bf 109 on 24 March 1945 – he also claimed two strafing victories, hence the eight kill symbols on 44-64051. All of his success came in this aircraft.

After the war Evans remained in the air force and commanded the 49th Fighter Bomber Wing during the Korean War, and he was shot down and captured on 27 March 1953. Later, he commanded the Seventh and Thirteenth Air Forces in Thailand during the Vietnam War. Evans finally retired in 1973 as a major general. 44-64051 was one of a number of surplus USAAF P-51D/Ks supplied to the Italian air force post-war.

29

P-51D-15 44-15888 *WHOLE HAWG* of Maj Donald McGee, 363rd FS, Leiston, March 1945

Don McGee became an ace with the 8th FG over New Guinea, flying with both the 36th and 80th FSs. He downed five Japanese aircraft (three A6Ms, a G4M1 and a Ki-61) while flying P-39s, P-40s and P-38s in 1942-43. Having completed 154 combat missions, McGee returned home in November 1943 and became a P-47 instructor. However, he eventually volunteered for another combat tour and joined the 357th FG in September 1944. Given command of the 363rd FS in January 1945, McGee scored his final victory, over a Bf 109, on 2 March 1945 near Magdeburg in this aircraft. McGee also led the 364th FS in the final days of World War 2 and immediately post-war.

30

P-51D-20 44-63199 *TOOLIN' FOOL'S REVENGE* of Lt Otto Jenkins, 362nd FS, Leiston, March 1945

Otto Jenkins flew this fighter between mid-January and late March 1945, but he did not score any of his kills with it. While returning from the final mission of his tour on 24 March, Jenkins buzzed Leiston in 44-63199 and clipped trees, crashing to his death. Ironically, the original *TOOLIN' FOOL* (P-51D-5 44-13735) had also crashed, losing a wing while chasing German fighters near Naumberg and killing Maj Lawrence Giarrizzo on 2 November 1944.

31

P-51D-20 44-72244 of Maj Donald Bochkay, 363rd FS, Leiston, April 1945

Donald Bochkay, a native of North Hollywood, California, served with the 357th FG from its establishment and destroyed 13.833 enemy aircraft. He was among the very few pilots to count two Me 262s among his victories. Bochkay was assigned this aircraft after his previous mount, 44-15422, suffered a coolant system failure and was force-landed by Lt John Casey on 15 February. On 18 April 1945, Bochkay scored his final kill while flying this machine, which survived the war.

32

P-51D-5 44-11190 *LADY OVELLA* of Capt John Sublett, 362nd FS, Leiston, April, 1945

John Sublett, another former instructor posted to the 357th FG in the autumn of 1944, opened his score in spectacular fashion shortly after his arrival with a triple kill haul in this machine on 27 November 1944. He became an ace by downing two enemy fighters on 14 January 1945, again in 44-11190, and he shot down three more in March. *LADY OVELLA* was lost in a crash on 21 May 1945 southwest of Ipswich that killed the pilot, Lt Alfred Bierweiler.

33

P-51D-20 44-72199 of Capt Charles Weaver, 362nd FS, Leiston, April 1945

As previously mentioned, 'Chuck' Weaver initially inherited wingman Arval Roberson's *Passion WAGON* at the end of the latter's tour, so there was some precedent for large nude figures being displayed on his Mustangs. Weaver's next aircraft had no name, but it did feature what was possibly the most striking nose art of any 357th FG aircraft. On 18 April 1945, Weaver was flying this machine when he destroyed an Me 262 over Prague-Ruzyne airfield. He finished the war with eight kills, achieved during 73 missions. 44-72199 was supplied to the Swiss air force in 1948.

34

P-51D-5 44-13783 *ROVIN' RHODA/4 BOLTS* of Lt Irving Snedeker, 364th FS, Leiston, April 1945

This aircraft began its career as Lt George Morris' *Bobby Marilyn* before being allocated to Irving Snedeker, who scored a kill on 'Big Day'. While strafing Prague-Ruzyne airfield on 17 April 1945, a flak shell took away the aircraft's spinner and propeller and Snedeker was forced to belly-in within the perimeter of the field. He climbed from the wreck, sat down some distance away, lit a cigarette and waited to be captured. Held initially at the base, he was entertained by Me 262 pilots who joked with him about flying 'obsolete propeller aeroplanes'. Snedeker was transferred to the local jail, but was soon returned to the base. With the Russians approaching, Snedeker was told that he was the senior American officer in the area, and the base was duly surrendered to him!

35

P-51K-5 44-11678 *BOBBY JEANNE/Ah Fung-Goo* of Col Irwin Dregne, CO of the 357th FG, Leiston, April 1945

A native of Viroqua, Wisconsin, Irwin Dregne commanded the 357th FG from 2 December 1944 until 21 July 1945, during which time he destroyed five enemy aircraft (two in the air and three on the ground) – the last two in this aircraft. The name *BOBBY JEANNE* referred to Dregne's wife and daughter, while *Ah Fung-Goo* was chosen by the crew chief. Dregne was an original member of the group, but he briefly served with the 363rd FG as its Operations Officer between March and May 1943. Returning to the 357th FG, he would eventually become its final wartime CO.

36

P-51D-20 44-64099 *ARKANSAS TRAVELLER* of Capt Thomas Adams, 364th FS, Leiston, April 1945

Thomas Adams was another late arrival, reporting for service with the group in December 1944 and achieving 4.5 aerial and one strafing victories by war's end. He made up for his late start with a kill on 5 December, then shared a victory with Irving Snedeker near Kassel on 5 January. An aerial kill and a strafing victory on 10 January were followed by two Fw 190s shot down during 'Big Day'.

INDEX